THE SELF LOVE GUIDE

MASTER TECHNIQUES TO OVERCOME LOW SELF-ESTEEM, QUIET SELF-DOUBT, AND CRUSH NEGATIVE SELF-TALK

EMBARK ON YOUR JOURNEY TOWARD YOUR BEST YOU

WILLOW.CEDAR.SAGE COLLECTIVE

CONTENTS

INTRODUCTION

Have you ever stopped to consider what self-love truly means in your life? This question often gets overlooked because of our busy lives and societal pressures. But, pondering this could lead to a transformative journey that can profoundly change your views on happiness, strength, and resilience. Self-love isn't just about pampering yourself; it's about grounding your entire being in respect and affection that radiates outward, affecting every aspect of your life.

This book is not simply a collection of theories and techniques; it's a testament to a personal journey. A journey that began when I realized my self-love was conditional, tied to achievements and the opinions of others. This revelation shook my world, propelling me toward a more authentic and nurturing relationship with myself. As a life and wellness coach, I've had the privilege of guiding others on this path, helping them find their inner sanctuary of self-respect and care. It is from these interactions and personal revelations that *The Self Love Guide* was born.

What sets this book apart is its interactive nature. It's not just a theoretical exploration; it's a practical guide that will accompany you step-by-step on your journey to self-love. Each chapter is crafted to deepen your understanding and practice of self-love, with workbook and journaling prompts that encourage you to reflect and engage with the material. This interactive aspect will genuinely enrich your journey.

Engaging with this book will uncover the tools to boost your self-esteem, conquer doubts, and embrace your imperfections as hidden strengths. You'll learn how to foster resilience and transform how you face life's challenges. More importantly, you'll discover how to celebrate yourself every single day.

As you embark on this journey, remember that you're not alone. You're joining a vibrant community of fellow seekers, all striving to foster a kinder, more loving relationship with themselves. This community is not just a concept; it's a tangible support system. You'll find support and inspiration through online forums and social media, reminding you that you are not alone in this quest.

I invite you to approach this book with an open heart and a curious mind. Let it be a safe space to explore, question, and grow. As we start, I encourage you to reflect: What does self-love mean to you right now, and what do you hope it will mean by the end of this journey?

Let's begin this beautiful exploration together, nurturing a love that starts within and radiates so powerfully outward, reshaping our lives in ways we might never have imagined.

CHAPTER ONE
UNDERSTANDING SELF-LOVE

Have you ever had a moment when you looked in the mirror and felt a genuine sense of self-appreciation, not for your appearance but for who you are as a person? Though these moments may seem as rare as finding a four-leaf clover, they are the essence of true self-love. This chapter is not just about the concept of self-love but about how it can transform your life. It's about moving beyond societal expectations and embracing your true self, shifting your focus from the external to the internal, from appearance to essence.

Self-love is a term often tossed around these days, sandwiched between the latest wellness trends and motivational hashtags. But when you strip away all the buzz, what remains is a concept that is both profoundly simple and deeply complex. It's about nurturing a relationship with yourself that's as caring and unconditional as the one you'd hope to have with a life partner or a close friend. Yes, it can be as challenging as climbing a mountain backward, but remember, you are not just capable of climbing that mountain; *you are the mountain itself,* and self-love is within your reach.

Let's unpack this together, shall we?

1.1 BEYOND THE MIRROR: DEFINING SELF-LOVE IN YOUR LIFE

When discussing self-love, the first image that might pop into your head could be a pampered spa day or a shopping spree. But here's the thing: self-love isn't just about feeling good on the outside. It's about appreciating who you are on the inside. This kind of love transcends physical appearance and deepens into a holistic appreciation of oneself.

Think about the last time you achieved something significant. You could have aced a test, won a game, or got praised at work. It felt good, right? But here's a twist—true self-love isn't conditional on these achievements or external validations. It's about knowing your worth even when everything seems to go wrong. It's understanding that your value isn't tied to your successes or failures.

Embracing self-love is not a destination but a continuous journey. It's a practice that evolves as you grow, requiring dedication to self-compassion. This means being as kind to yourself as you would be to a friend in their time of need. It's about catching those harsh self-criticisms you throw at yourself and challenging them with kindness and truth. This practice reminds you, time and again, that you are enough. Remember, self-love is not a one-time event but a lifelong commitment to yourself, a journey of self-discovery and personal growth that inspires and motivates you.

Self-love is not just about feeling good; it's about setting and maintaining boundaries that protect your well-being. It's like building a beautiful garden around your life—only those who respect the garden's rules are welcome. These boundaries are not walls to keep people out but rather fences safeguarding your peace. They help you prioritize your well-being and make choices that genuinely benefit you, not just please others. Self-love is your tool for creating a safe and nurturing environment for yourself.

Interactive Element: Self-Love Reflection

Take a moment to reflect on this: How do you treat yourself when things don't go as planned? Do you criticize yourself harshly, or do you offer words of comfort? Try writing down what you typically say to yourself in challenging times and then rewrite these thoughts with kindness and compassion. This exercise can help you begin to transform your inner dialogue into one that supports and nurtures you, just as you deserve.

1.2 THE HISTORY OF SELF-LOVE: LEARNING FROM THE PAST TO SHAPE OUR FUTURE

Isn't it fascinating how concepts evolve over time? Let's take a stroll down history lane, where the roots of self-love stretch deep into the soil of ancient civilizations and weave through various cultural tapestries to emerge in today's modern therapy sessions and Instagram feeds. The journey of self-love isn't a trend that popped up out of nowhere; it's a rich, evolving narrative that reflects the shifting landscapes of societal values and the understanding of genuinely caring for oneself.

In ancient times, self-love was not just a personal indulgence but a crucial element of societal well-being. Societies like Greece and Rome intertwined self-love with self-care, advocating for physical training, philosophical pondering, and spiritual rituals. The Greeks had a word for this: "philautia," which translates to "love of self." Aristotle said that in order to achieve true happiness, one must have an appropriate amount of self-love. This was a balanced love, not veering into vanity or self-obsession, but rather a love that fueled personal growth and broader societal contributions. This historical context underscores the importance of self-love in our personal growth and societal contributions.

Further illustrating the ancient embrace of self-care, Egyptian civilization regarded cleanliness and physical upkeep as integral to personal and spiritual purity, caring for your physical body was linked to maintaining moral and societal integrity. Similarly, in Eastern traditions, practices like yoga and meditation developed to foster self-awareness and inner peace, forms of self-love that focus on harmonizing the body, mind, and spirit.

Transitioning into the Renaissance, focusing on individualism brought about a different kind of self-reflection. This era revived many Classical ideas and infused them with contemporary flavors; it highlighted each person's ability and the need for individual health and happiness as a foundation for improving society. From these seeds, modern concepts of self-love began to sprout, branching out through the ages as societies grew more complex.

Now, let's zoom into more recent times, where the industrial and post-industrial periods brought about drastic changes in how communities functioned. The rise of psychology as a field in the late 19th and early 20th centuries marked a pivotal shift in understanding human behavior and mental health. Figures like William James and, later, Carl Rogers and Abraham Maslow began exploring self-esteem and self-actualization, laying the groundwork for today's self-love movements. These pioneers taught us that self-love isn't just about feeling good about oneself—it's about recognizing and fulfilling one's potential, which in turn enriches the community at large.

As we enter the contemporary era, the conversation around self-love has become more inclusive and diversified. Movements across the globe advocate for mental health awareness, body positivity, and the breaking down of stigmas surrounding self-care. What's fascinating here is how self-love is becoming accessible to everyone.

It's no longer seen as a luxury reserved for the affluent or the spiritual elite but as a fundamental right and necessity for everyone. For all its pitfalls, social media has played a significant role in this, offering platforms where diverse groups can share their struggles and successes, fostering a community of support and acceptance.

Each of these historical shifts brings us valuable lessons about the nature of self-love. They show us that as societies evolve, so does our understanding of what it means to love and care for ourselves. They remind us that self-love is not static; it's a dynamic force that has the power to shape not only individual lives but the fabric of society itself. By learning from these past attitudes and practices, we can better navigate the complexities of modern life and use self-love as a tool for personal and societal well-being.

Reflecting on this rich history, it becomes clear why self-love is more crucial today than ever before. In a rapidly changing world where external pressures and media influences constantly bombard us, grounding ourselves in the practice of self-love provides not just a shield but a nurturing force, helping us to thrive amidst chaos. It's not just about surviving the storm; it's about learning to dance in the rain, embracing every drop, and knowing that each one nourishes and strengthens us in its own way.

1.3 DEBUNKING MYTHS: WHAT SELF-LOVE IS AND ISN'T

So, let's clear the air about a few misconceptions floating around like those annoying fruit flies that won't leave your kitchen. We must address these myths head-on because, let's face it, misunderstanding self-love can muddy the waters of how we treat ourselves and understand our worth. One of the biggest myths out there is equating self-love with being selfish. How many times have you heard someone say, or maybe even thought to yourself, that taking time for yourself is a selfish act? This myth is sticky, but it's about as accurate as the five-second rule (and let's be honest, we've all eaten that cookie off the floor after a bit longer).

Self-love is not about neglecting others for your own gain; it's about healthy self-respect. Think about it this way: when you're on an airplane, they always tell you to put your oxygen mask on first before helping others. Why? Because you can't pour from an empty cup (or breathe from an empty tank if we're sticking with the airplane analogy). Prioritizing your well-being isn't about saying you matter more than others; it's about acknowledging that you matter, too. It's about giving yourself permission to thrive so that you can help others do the same.

Now, onto the next big myth: self-love as a gateway to narcissism. There's a common belief that self-love might turn you into a self-absorbed person who can't see beyond their reflection in the mirror. But here's the twist—real self-love is actually a breeding ground for empathy and compassion. It's pretty straightforward when you think about it: understanding and forgiving yourself allows you to extend that same kindness to others. When you recognize your own flaws and struggles, you're more likely to empathize with the struggles of those around you. It's the difference between seeing someone trip and helping them up versus laughing and walking away. Real self-love enhances our connection to others; it doesn't diminish it.

Another myth that needs busting is the idea that self-love is a static state—like you reach a point of self-love and boom, you're done, forever basking in self-admiration. But self-love isn't a trophy on a shelf. It's more like a muscle that needs regular workouts to stay strong. It grows and evolves with you over time. Some days, loving yourself might mean saying no to an extra workload; others might mean pushing yourself to go for that morning jog because you know it makes you feel alive. The dynamic nature of self-love means that it adapts to fit your needs and circumstances at any given moment in your life.

Debunking these myths is more than just setting the record straight; it's a crucial step in allowing ourselves and others to embrace self-love without the baggage of guilt or misunderstanding. It's about creating a culture where self-love is seen as what it truly is: a vital part of a healthy, balanced life. By understanding what self-love really means, we can start to practice it in a way that enriches our lives and the lives of those around us. It's about stripping away the misconceptions and getting to the heart of self-love—caring for and respecting ourselves in a way that reflects our inherent worth.

As we wrap up this chapter, let's carry forward this clearer understanding of self-love, not as a self-centered act nor a fixed state of being but a dynamic and compassionate practice that enriches our lives. It's time to shake off the old views and breathe new life into our relationship with ourselves. As we do so, let's remember that each step we take in understanding and practicing true self-love is a step toward personal contentment and fostering a more empathetic and supportive world. So, keep this newfound knowledge close as you move forward, allowing it to light your path to deeper self-awareness and greater self-kindness.

Please refer to the "Journal Prompts" section at the end of the book and follow the prompts for Chapter 1.

CHAPTER TWO

THE SCIENCE AND SOUL OF SELF-LOVE

Have you ever wondered why you feel like a weight has been lifted off your shoulders after a hearty laugh with friends or a good cry during a sappy movie? Or why, when you finally forgive yourself for a past mistake, do you almost physically feel lighter? Well, there's a scientific symphony at play behind these experiences, and it's all happening in your brain. Let's peel back the layers of our minds and explore how understanding the psychology behind self-love can radically enhance our lives.

Imagine your brain as this incredibly complex, bustling city with neurons zooming around like cars, forming freeways of thoughts, emotions, and reactions. Now, what happens in this neural metropolis when you practice self-love? Spoiler alert: it's all good news. From the quiet suburbs of your cerebral cortex to the bustling downtown of your limbic system, self-love sends ripples of positive change throughout this city, laying down new roads and improving old ones. Let's dive deep into how kindness to yourself actually rewires the brain and why this neurological remodeling is something you'd want to sign up for.

2.1 THE PSYCHOLOGY BEHIND SELF-LOVE: WHY YOUR BRAIN NEEDS KINDNESS

Neuroscientific Makeover: Rewiring with Self-Compassion

Have you ever felt that loop of negative self-talk, where one bad thought leads to another until it feels like a never-ending spiral? That's your brain following well-trodden neural pathways. The good news? Neuroplasticity is your brain's innate ability to change and adapt in response to new experiences—which means you can reroute those pathways. Studies in neuroscience have shown that practices of self-compassion and kindness can physically change the structure and function of your brain. When you engage in self-love, you're not just feeling better in that moment; you're funda-mentally rewiring your brain to handle stress and anxiety more effectively. This isn't just fluffy talk—it's backed by science. Regular acts of self-kindness can strengthen areas of the brain associated with positive emotions and weaken those linked to negative emotions, making resilience more than just a buzzword.

Psychological Theories: Building Blocks of Self-Actualization

The journey to self-love aligns beautifully with several psycholog-ical theories, particularly Maslow's hierarchy of needs. Introduced by psychologist Abraham Maslow in the 1940s, this theory is often visualized as a pyramid and serves as a framework for under-standing human motivation. At the base of the pyramid are physio-logical needs—basic necessities like food, water, and shelter. Once these are satisfied, the next level addresses safety needs, which include security, stability, and freedom from fear.

Moving up the pyramid, the next layer involves social needs, which encompass love, belonging, and relationships. It's here that self-love begins to play a crucial role. By cultivating a deep love and acceptance of oneself, you not only meet these social needs in your own life but also create a stable foundation for further growth. Essentially, nurturing self-love sets up a 'base camp' from which you can embark on the higher pursuits of the pyramid.

The following level includes esteem needs, which involve achieving respect, status, and recognition and developing feelings of self-esteem and personal worth. Self-love enhances this layer by reinforcing a positive self-image and confidence, paving the way for you to pursue and achieve your goals.

At the pinnacle of Maslow's pyramid sits self-actualization—the fulfillment of one's potential and the pursuit of personal growth, creativity, and peak experiences. Maslow believed that reaching this stage was the ultimate goal of human development. However, there's an intriguing twist: before you can even think about reaching this peak, all the foundational needs, including love and belonging, must be met. This is where self-love becomes crucial. By embracing and nurturing love for yourself, you satisfy these fundamental needs, creating a solid foundation for personal growth and happiness. This sense of fulfillment and contentment is a direct result of self-love.

Thus, embracing self-love does more than fill an emotional void; it creates a robust platform for continual personal development. With each step on this pyramid that self-love strengthens, you gain a more hopeful and motivating outlook on life, making the climb toward self-actualization not just possible but enjoyable. This journey through Maslow's hierarchy with self-love as your guide shows how deeply interconnected our psychological needs are with the practice of loving oneself.

Emotional Resilience: Your Inner Shock Absorber

Think of emotional resilience as your psychological shock absorber. Life will inevitably throw potholes and speed bumps your way, but self-love equips you with the resilience to navigate these with fewer scrapes and bruises. When you cultivate a loving and forgiving relationship with yourself, you're better prepared to bounce back from setbacks. This resilience stems from a deep-seated belief in your own worth and capabilities. It's like having an emotional first aid kit; whenever you face adversity, you can patch yourself up faster and keep moving forward, making you feel stronger and more prepared for life's challenges.

Self-Perception: The Mirror and The Mind

Understanding the brain's role in self-perception can be a game-changer in your self-love practice. Our brains are not passive observers but active architects of our reality, including how we see ourselves. When you shift toward a more compassionate self-view, you're essentially giving your brain a new job highlighting your positive qualities and contributions rather than letting it default to criticism and doubt. This doesn't mean ignoring your flaws but rather viewing them through a lens of understanding and growth.

Interactive Element: Reflective Journaling Prompt

Here's a practical exercise to incorporate self-love into your daily life: for the next week, before you sleep, jot down three things you forgave yourself for. These could be mistakes, missed opportunities, or instances when you were too hard on yourself. This simple practice can shift your brain's focus from self-criticism to self-compassion, reinforcing the neural pathways that promote resilience and well-being.

2.2 EMOTIONAL INTELLIGENCE: THE HEART OF SELF-LOVE

Have you ever met someone who seems to handle every high and low with a kind of grace that almost feels like they've got an emotional superpower? Well, let me let you in on a not-so-secret secret: that superpower is likely emotional intelligence (EI), a critical component in the toolkit of self-love. Emotional intelligence isn't just about controlling your emotions or always staying positive; it's about navigating your feelings in a way that helps you understand yourself better and improves how you connect with others.

Imagine you're sitting in a café, sipping your favorite coffee, and out of nowhere, a wave of anxiety hits you because of an upcoming meeting. If you're equipped with a tuned EI, instead of letting this anxiety spiral out of control, you would recognize these feelings, understand their source, and decide how best to address them. Maybe you take deep breaths, text a friend, or jot down your thoughts in a journal. Here, emotional intelligence acts as a buffer against distress and a bridge to better self-management.

This ability to manage our emotions is crucial, especially when the seas of life get stormy. It's easy to be kind to ourselves when everything is smooth sailing, but the real test comes during storms. That's where self-regulation comes into play. This aspect of EI involves controlling or redirecting our disruptive emotions and adapting to changes with flexibility. It doesn't mean suppressing your feelings—it's about expressing them appropriately so they don't derail your self-esteem or your day. Mastering this can transform your relationship with yourself from criticism and frustration to encouragement and forgiveness.

Now, let's talk about self-awareness, another jewel in the crown of emotional intelligence. This is all about clearly understanding your emotions, strengths, weaknesses, drives, and values. When you know what makes you tick, you can manage impulses, communicate more effectively, and maintain your professionalism, even in challenging situations. For instance, if you're aware that you're prone to stress eating, acknowledging this can help you develop healthier coping strategies. Or, if you know that you're particularly sensitive to criticism, you can work on strategies to receive feedback in a way that fosters growth rather than resentment.

But emotional intelligence isn't just about looking inward; it's also about how you connect with others. It enhances your social skills, helping you navigate relationships' complexities with empathy and understanding. When you're emotionally intelligent, you're not just tuned into your own emotions; you're also sensitive to the feelings and needs of others. This makes you a better friend, partner, colleague, or leader. For example, imagine your friend is going through a tough time. With high EI, you might pick up on subtleties in their mood that others might miss and offer support in a genuinely helpful way instead of just going through the motions.

Emotional intelligence ultimately serves as a cornerstone in the architecture of self-love. It equips you with the tools to face personal challenges with a calm mind and a compassionate heart. Moreover, it empowers you to forge deeper connections with others, enriching your life's tapestry with relationships that are rooted in mutual respect and understanding. As you continue to explore and enhance your emotional intelligence, remember each step forward is a step toward a more fulfilled, emotionally balanced you, where every emotion is acknowledged, every challenge is gracefully navigated, and every relationship is cherished.

2.3 THE RIPPLE EFFECT: HOW SELF-LOVE BENEFITS THOSE AROUND US

Imagine yourself as a pebble thrown into a vast, still lake. The moment you hit the surface, you create a ripple; it starts small but quickly spreads far and wide, touching distant shores you might not even see. Now, picture that pebble as your practice of self-love. Every act of kindness and acceptance toward yourself doesn't just uplift you; it starts a ripple effect, influencing others around you and, ultimately, contributing to a more loving society.

Let's break down how this happens. Think about the days when you feel good about yourself, filled with self-love and inner peace. You're more likely to smile at a stranger, compliment a friend genuinely, or offer a helping hand without a second thought. These acts might seem small, but they carry weight. They can turn someone's bad day around or even inspire them to pass on the kindness. This is the contagious nature of self-love in action. It's not just about feeling good but spreading that goodness around like your favorite jam on a slice of warm, toasty bread.

Now, the societal impact of widespread self-love could be monumental. In a world where self-criticism and comparison are the norm, fostering an environment that celebrates self-compassion and acceptance could be revolutionary. By nurturing love for ourselves, we set a standard for how we treat others. This creates a culture where empathy and understanding are reflexes, not afterthoughts. Consider how different daily interactions would be if everyone you met were secure in their self-worth and not driven by hidden insecurities or competitive impulses. This shift could dismantle some of the toxic standards that society upholds, replacing them with values that promote genuine well-being and happiness.

Moreover, you naturally establish healthier boundaries when you respect and love yourself. You recognize your worth and understand where you end and others begin. This clarity allows you to interact with others more effectively. It's like knowing exactly how much weight you can lift; avoiding taking on too much might avoid resentment or exhaustion. People around you will notice and often mirror this respect, leading to more balanced and fulfilling relationships. It's like a dance where everyone knows the steps and moves together harmoniously rather than stepping on each other's toes.

If more people viewed themselves and others through a lens of compassion and acceptance, societal norms could shift away from judgment and exclusion toward inclusivity and support. This change can ripple out further than we might imagine, touching everything from mental health stigmas to workplace dynamics, educational approaches, and policy-making. The potential for positive change is as boundless as the ripples from our proverbial pebble.

So, as you turn the pages of this chapter, think of each page as a ripple you're creating in the lake of your community. Your journey of self-love is not just about you. It's about setting into motion waves of change that can transform the world into a kinder, more compassionate place. What starts with you doesn't end with you; it echoes outwards, touching lives and reshaping norms.

As we wrap up this exploration of the ripple effects of self-love, let's pause and reflect on the powerful impact our personal attitudes and behaviors can have on the broader canvas of society. Each act of self-love fortifies our emotional resilience and contributes to a cultural shift toward greater empathy and acceptance. By fostering an environment where self-love is celebrated and encouraged, we participate in a collective movement that can dismantle toxic norms and pave the way for a more inclusive and supportive society. Keep this vision in mind as we transition into the next chapter, where we will delve deeper into the practical strategies and daily practices that can help us cultivate and sustain self-love in our lives. Let's continue to create ripples that inspire and uplift, forging a path toward a more loving and compassionate world.

Please refer to the "Journal Prompts" section at the end of the book and follow the prompts for Chapter 2.

CHAPTER THREE
YOUR SELF-LOVE STARTING LINE

Have you ever had that moment when you're about to draw a self-portrait, and just before the pencil hits the paper, you pause? Suddenly, you're not just thinking about which features to sketch or what expression to capture, but also how you truly see yourself. This chapter is kind of like that moment of pause—only instead of sketching with a pencil, we're going to sketch a clearer picture of your self-love with some honest reflection. It's about peeking into your internal mirror, not to scrutinize or criticize, but to observe and understand. Ready to take a peek? Let's start by figuring out where you truly stand on your self-love path.

3.1 WHERE ARE YOU NOW? A SELF-LOVE ASSESSMENT

Understanding Your Current State: The Self-Love Litmus Test

First off, let's do a little self-love litmus test. Think of it not as a test you could fail but as a way to gauge what kind of self-love nutrients might be in short supply. How do you typically react to setbacks? Do you treat yourself harshly or with kindness? When you achieve something, do you give yourself a mental high-five, or is it never quite good enough? Your answers aren't just responses; they're clues. They help peel back the layers of daily habits and long-held beliefs to reveal how deeply you cherish and respect yourself.

Reflecting on your past can sometimes feel like opening an old diary—each memory a page etched with emotions. It's a task many of us shy away from, perhaps because revisiting the past can bring discomfort or even pain. However, engaging with these memories is crucial. They help you pinpoint moments that shaped your current self-perception. Maybe it was the relentless pursuit of perfection in school or a harsh critique from someone you admired. These experiences, especially the challenging ones, are like knots in the thread of your self-love. Recognizing them helps you under-stand where you might need to loosen the knots and smooth the thread, allowing you to heal and move forward with a clearer, kinder view of yourself.

Now, here comes a fun part—recognizing your strengths and accomplishments. Often, we overlook our victories, big or small, without a second thought. But here, please pause and give yourself that applause you skipped. Maybe you helped a friend through a tough time, mastered a new recipe, or stood up for something you believed in. Each of these moments is a building block of your self-love. They're proof of your kindness, skill, bravery, and much more. Stack them up, and you'll start to see the foundation of a solid self-love structure.

Interactive Element: The Self-Love Mapping Exercise

Let's put this into practice. Grab a sheet of paper, or open a new digital note, and draw a simple map. Start with a dot labeled "You Are Here." From there, draw lines leading out to different areas of your life—relationships, work, passions, health. Along each line, jot down brief notes on how you feel about yourself in these areas. Be honest, but also be kind. This map isn't just showing you where you are; it's helping you chart a course to where you want to be.

As you sketch out your self-love map, think about the areas that need more attention. Maybe you're great at supporting friends but not so kind to yourself. Or perhaps you're a star at work but struggle to give yourself downtime. These aren't just observations; they're signposts pointing you toward your next steps in your self-love adventure.

In crafting this map, you're doing more than just doodling. You're taking the first crucial step in a more profound self-love practice. It's about setting realistic and meaningful goals tailored just for you to guide you toward a more prosperous, more loving relationship with yourself. As you continue exploring and adjusting your map, remember it's always in pencil, never pen. You can redraw, adjust, and expand it as you grow and learn more about the beautiful landscape of you.

Remember, this map is not fixed; it's a living document that will evolve as you do. So keep it handy, revisit it often, and allow it to guide you as you navigate the ever-changing terrain of your life. With each step, you're moving forward and paving the way for a more loving, compassionate, and fulfilling journey with yourself.

3.2 SETTING YOUR INTENTIONS: PERSONAL GOALS FOR SELF-LOVE

Imagine you're setting out on a road trip to a destination you've always wanted to explore. You wouldn't just jump in the car and drive off without a map, would you? Similarly, cultivating self-love isn't about wandering aimlessly in hopes of stumbling upon enlightenment—it's about setting clear intentions, like plotting your route on a map, ensuring each step moves you closer to where you want to be. These intentions act as your compass, guiding you with purpose and clarity, ensuring every choice and action enriches your relationship with yourself.

Setting intentions for self-love is much like planting seeds in a garden. You decide what flowers or veggies you want to grow based on the harvest you're hoping for. Similarly, when you set intentions based on your core values—those deep-seated beliefs that define who you are—they ensure your self-love path is authentic and true to who you are at your core. For instance, if one of your core values is creativity, your intentions might involve dedicating time each week to paint, write, or create music, nurturing your creative spirit as an act of self-love.

Now, let's talk about the nature of your goals on this path. It's easy to fall into the trap of setting rigid, high-stakes goals that leave no room for the ebb and flow of daily life. But here's a little secret: the most nourishing intentions are those that are flexible and compassionate. Life is unpredictable and ever-changing, so your goals for self-love should be adaptable, allowing for growth and change as you evolve. This flexibility means that if you hit a bump or take a detour, you can adjust your course without harsh judgment, treating these moments as opportunities for learning and growth rather than failures. This journey is in your hands, empowering you to shape it as you see fit.

Imagine this scenario: you set an intention to meditate every morning to cultivate inner peace and self-awareness. A family crisis throws your schedule off balance one week, and you miss a few sessions. Being flexible means you can change your plans when needed—maybe you shorten your meditation sessions or shift them to the evening—rather than dropping them entirely or beating yourself up. This adaptability in your goals keeps the spirit of self-love alive, turning "failures" into just another part of your growth story.

Furthermore, the journey of self-love is filled with small victories that often go unnoticed. Maybe you chose a healthy meal over fast food, stood up for yourself in a difficult conversation, or took a few minutes to breathe deeply amidst a busy day. These moments might seem small, but they are profound victories in the art of self-care. Celebrating these wins is crucial because acknowledgment reinforces your efforts and motivates you to continue. It's like giving yourself a high-five; it boosts your morale and reminds you that you're making progress, no matter how incremental it might seem.

To truly celebrate these victories, make a habit of reflecting on your day or week to identify these moments. You could keep a victory jar where you drop notes about these wins or make a weekly victory post on social media to share your progress with friends. Each celebration is a reaffirmation of your commitment to self-love and a reminder that every step forward, no matter how small, is a step toward a more loving relationship with yourself.

In setting your intentions for self-love, remember they are not just checklists to be marked off. They are profound commitments to treating yourself with kindness, respect, and compassion, steering you toward a life where self-love is not just an occasional luxury but a constant, nurturing presence. As you continue to define and refine these intentions, let your deepest values guide them, be flexible in their design, and celebrate at every possible turn, enriching your life with every conscious step you take.

3.3 CRAFTING YOUR SELF-LOVE AFFIRMATION MANTRA

Ever wake up feeling like the world's got a gray filter on? You know, those days when you spill coffee on your shirt, miss an important email, and just can't catch a break? On days like these, a personal self-love affirmation mantra can be your secret weapon. Think of it as your very own cheerleader, tucked in your pocket, ready to remind you of your worth and resilience, no matter how topsy-turvy the world seems.

Affirmations are powerful tools; they're like verbal vitamins that boost your mental and emotional health. Every time you repeat your mantra, it's not just words that you're saying. You're reinforcing a belief in your abilities and worth. It's like laying down a new track over those old, worn-out records of self-doubt and criticism that play in your mind. Over time, these affirmations can reshape your thought patterns, turning knee-jerk self-criticism into instinctive self-compassion. This isn't just fluffy science; it's backed by neuroplasticity, the brain's ability to rewire itself. By affirming positive beliefs, you're literally changing the wiring in your brain, fostering a mindset that embraces self-love and confidence.

Creating your own self-love affirmation mantra is like writing a love letter to yourself. It should be personal, meaningful, and uplifting. Start by identifying what qualities you admire about yourself or areas where you seek growth. It could be your creativity, determination, or ability to find joy in small things. Perhaps you aim to be more patient with yourself or embrace your imperfections. Whatever it is, let it shape your affirmation. For instance, if you're focusing on self-acceptance, your mantra might be something like, "I am enough, just as I am." If resilience is your goal, try, "I am strong, I overcome." The key is to keep it positive, present tense, and punchy—something you can say easily, no matter where you are or what you're doing.

Integrating these affirmations into your daily routine can be surprisingly simple and incredibly effective. Stick a post-it note on your mirror with your mantra so it's the first thing you see in the morning. Or set a daily alarm with your affirmation as the label, turning a mundane moment into a mini self-love ritual. You can even use your mantra as a password or PIN code—imagine reinforcing your self-love every time you unlock your phone or log into an account! The more you repeat your affirmation, the more ingrained it becomes in your consciousness, steadily shifting your self-perception toward something profoundly positive.

But why keep all this goodness to yourself? Sharing your mantra with others can amplify its power. It's like lighting candles from a single flame; you spread light and warmth without dimming your own. When you share your affirmations, you invite others to reflect on their own qualities and aspirations. It creates a ripple effect of positivity and self-love that can uplift an entire community. Whether through social media, a blog, or just a conversation with friends, opening up about your self-love practice can inspire others to embark on their own. Plus, it strengthens your commitment to your mantra, embedding it even deeper into your daily life.

As you craft and use your self-love affirmation mantra, remember it's more than just a string of words. It's a declaration of your intrinsic value and a step toward embracing yourself with kindness and respect. Each repetition is a brick in the foundation of your self-esteem, building a resilient structure where you can grow and flourish. So, create that mantra, and let it be a beacon that guides you through the foggy days and a celebration of who you are on the sunny days.

As we wrap up this chapter on beginning your self-love practices, remember that the journey to loving yourself more profoundly is both challenging and rewarding. It requires honesty, commitment, and, most importantly, a gentle approach. From assessing where you stand and setting meaningful intentions to crafting affirmations that resonate with your soul, each step is integral. They weave together to form a stronger, more loving relationship with yourself. As you move forward, carry these tools with you, ready to deepen your self-love and spread its warmth to others. In the next chapter, we will explore how embracing your imperfections can actually enhance your self-love practice, turning every flaw into a milestone of your unique journey.

Please refer to the "Journal Prompts" section at the end of the book and follow the prompts for Chapter 3.

CHAPTER FOUR

EMBRACING IMPERFECTION

Ever look at a handmade ceramic bowl, noticing how its uneven edges and unpredictable glaze make it stunningly beautiful? There's something about its perfect imperfection that draws you in, right? Think of yourself as that bowl. Like those quirky, uneven lines add character to the pottery, your flaws and imperfections add depth and uniqueness to who you are. In this chapter, we will explore why striving for a glossy, magazine-cover version of perfection might be what's holding you back from truly shining. Let's crack the myth of perfection wide open and discover how our flaws are not just okay; they're actually superpowers in disguise.

4.1 PERFECTIONISM UNVEILED: WHY YOUR FLAWS ARE YOUR SUPERPOWERS

The Hidden Fear Behind the Perfect Facade

Why do we chase perfection like it's a train we're about to miss? Often, it's not about pursuing excellence but rather a shield against fear and insecurity. That relentless drive for perfection can be a smokescreen, masking our dread of criticism and rejection. It's as if we believe that by being perfect, we can protect ourselves from the pain of being seen as flawed. But here's the kicker: this pursuit can end up boxing us in, limiting our experiences and self-expression. When constantly worrying about maintaining a perfect façade, you will likely avoid taking risks or trying new things. After all, stepping into the unknown is messy and far from ideal.

Embrace Your Flaws: Unleashing Authenticity and Creativity

Now, imagine letting go of that exhausting strive for perfection. What if you viewed your quirks and imperfections not as liabilities but as assets? When you embrace your flaws, you open up a wellspring of creativity and authenticity. There's a reason why some of the most beloved pieces of art are those that defy conventional standards, capturing raw, unfiltered emotion. Your imperfections make you real, relatable, and uniquely you. They can fuel your creativity in surprising ways, leading to innovations and solutions that "perfect" could never achieve. By accepting and owning your flaws, you allow your true self to shine through and connect with others more genuinely—imperfections and all.

The Power Shift: From Self-Doubt to Empowerment

Viewing your imperfections as unique strengths is a radical shift in the narrative—from self-doubt to empowerment. This shift doesn't happen overnight, but it starts with changing the way you talk to yourself. Instead of beating yourself up over a mistake, what if you patted yourself on the back for trying? This reframing can transform your perspective, turning flaws into badges of courage and resilience. Every imperfection is a story of survival, a testament to your ability to adapt and overcome. When you start seeing your flaws through the lens of strength and survival, you empower yourself to take on challenges confidently, knowing that your imperfections are not roadblocks but stepping stones.

The Beauty in the Striving Process

Lastly, let's talk about the beauty in the process of striving itself. There's something profoundly beautiful about the act of striving—of reaching for something with all your heart, even if you never quite get there. The pursuit of perfection often robs us of appreciating this journey. We're so fixated on the flawless end result that we overlook the growth, learning, and joy that come from the act of trying. By letting go of the need for perfection, you can genuinely engage with the process, savoring each step, each mistake, and each triumph. This mindset not only makes the journey more enjoyable but also enriches your growth as you learn more from the process than you ever could from simply achieving a perfect end product.

Interactive Element: Journaling Prompt – "Embrace Your Flaws"

Take a moment to think deeply about three personal flaws or imperfections you've often criticized yourself for. This isn't a quick exercise; give yourself time to reflect on these aspects you might not usually appreciate. Next to each flaw, write down a positive aspect or strength that has emerged from it. For instance, if you've always felt that you were too sensitive, consider how this sensitivity makes you exceptionally empathetic and intuitive in your relationships. Alternatively, if you feel you're overly cautious, note how this trait has helped you make well-thought-out decisions. This exercise is about more than just listing qualities; it's about deeply understanding how what you perceive as weaknesses can also be your greatest strengths. By shifting your perspective in this way, you can start to embrace and celebrate these parts of yourself, recognizing them as unique strengths rather than shortcomings.

Embracing your imperfections isn't about lowering your standards or giving up on growth. It's about recognizing that true growth comes from authenticity, resilience, and the courage to be imperfect. As we continue to explore the nuances of self-love and acceptance, remember that your imperfections are not just obstacles to overcome; they are integral parts of the beautiful mosaic that makes up who you are. Let's cherish them as fiercely as we cherish our strengths, for they are what makes us genuinely human and irreplaceably individual.

4.2 STORIES OF IMPERFECTION: CELEBRATING OUR FLAWS

Have you ever noticed how stories of overcoming obstacles tend to stick with us much longer than tales of effortless success? Acknowledging our battles, especially those involving our imperfections, is incredibly human and profoundly relatable. History and our personal stories are rich with instances where what seemed like a disadvantage turned into a pivotal asset, leading to unexpected breakthroughs and profound personal triumphs.

Take, for instance, the world of art and science, where deviations from the norm have often paved the way for innovation. Consider the story of the famous Leaning Tower of Pisa. Initially, this unintended tilt was seen as a massive construction failure. Fast forward a few centuries, and this flaw has become the defining feature that attracts millions of tourists each year, turning a mistake into an iconic symbol of resilience and unique charm. Similar stories echo in the lives of many influential figures. Emily Dickinson, whose reclusive nature might have been seen as an imperfection, allowed her the solitude to create powerful poetry that continues to resonate with readers today. Her introspective nature transformed what could have been a limitation into a conduit for profound literary contributions.

Celebrating such imperfections in others does more than broaden our understanding; it fosters a culture of acceptance and empathy. When public figures openly share their struggles and unconventional traits, it challenges societal norms about what it means to be successful or "perfect." This openness humanizes them and makes the journey of self-acceptance less lonely for others. It sends a message that imperfections do not disqualify you from achieving greatness; instead, they are part of the mosaic that makes your story unique and your contributions valuable.

Sharing personal stories of imperfection can be equally transformative. When you open up about your struggles, whether it's about overcoming a learning disability, dealing with anxiety, or managing a failed project, you do more than just share a part of your life. You invite others into a safe space where they can relate, understand, and often find comfort in knowing they are not alone. This act of vulnerability can be powerful. It can turn your darkest moments into beacons of hope for someone else. Imagine you share a story about how you turned a major career setback into an opportunity to pursue a path you were genuinely passionate about. To someone standing at the crossroads of their career, your story might just be the push they need to explore new possibilities.

Moreover, recognizing how our imperfections contribute to our growth can revolutionize our self-perception. It shifts the internal narrative from one of self-criticism to one of kindness and under-standing. When you start to see your past errors not as failings but as integral steps in your learning process, you begin to treat your-self with more compassion. You learn to laugh at the times when you tripped over your own feet in a dance class or when you mispronounced a word during a presentation. Instead of blushing with embarrassment, you start to see these moments as points of growth and humor. This shift is not about dismissing the impor-tance of striving for improvement but about recognizing that growth often comes through imperfection, not in spite of it.

This new perspective is like watching the sunrise; it's slow and subtle but eventually fills your world with light. It teaches you that each flaw, stumble, and misstep is not a mark of defeat but a part of your evolution. As you continue to navigate through your own story, remember that your imperfections are not just obstacles to be overcome; they are opportunities to forge a deeper, more compas-sionate relationship with yourself and to inspire others to do the same.

4.3 FROM SELF-CRITICISM TO SELF-COMPASSION: TRANSFORMING YOUR INNER DIALOGUE

Let's face it: we all have that little voice in our heads that chimes in just when we mess up, telling us we could've done better or shouldn't have even tried. For many of us, this voice has been tuned by a lifetime of unrealistic standards and the relentless pres-sure to meet external expectations. It's like having a hyper-critical coach in your mind who doesn't know when to take a break. But what if you could transform that voice? What if, instead of tearing you down, it helped build you up?

The Birth of Self-Criticism: Unpacking the Pressure

Self-criticism often stems not from a place of genuine desire for self-improvement but from these towering, often unrealistic standards we set for ourselves. These standards are frequently sculpted by societal expectations, the glossy images on social media, or the accomplishments of those in our circles we admire. It's like constantly trying to reach a bar that's not just high; it's often in another stratosphere! This kind of mindset can lead us down a path of endless self-criticism. Every mistake is a catastrophe rather than a learning opportunity, and every success is lessened because it could have been 'better.' Recognizing the roots of these critical thoughts is the first step in transforming them. It involves a bit of detective work, tracing back these thoughts to understand whether they stem from your own values or from external pressures. This awareness creates a space between you and the criticism, a space where change can begin.

Kind Words, Kind Mind: Practicing Self-Compassion

Imagine speaking to a friend who has come to you disappointed by their own mistakes. Would you criticize them as you do yourself? Likely not. You'd probably offer kindness and understanding, perhaps pointing out what they could learn from the experience. This is the heart of self-compassion: treating yourself with the same kindness and understanding you'd offer a good friend. It's about acknowledging that making errors is not just human but a part of growth. When you falter, instead of jumping to criticism, you could gently remind yourself, "It's okay, everyone makes mistakes," or "Let's see what this teaches me." This softer, more supportive internal dialogue can dramatically shift your relationship with yourself from one of hostility to one of support.

*Techniques to Turn the Tide: Mindfulness and Cognitive
Restructuring*

Altering your inner dialogue from criticism to compassion might
sound great in theory, but how do you put it into practice?
Techniques like mindfulness and changing your thinking patterns
are here to help. Mindfulness helps you pay attention to your
thoughts and feelings without judging them. When you notice self-
critical thoughts, you acknowledge them and then let them pass
like clouds moving across the sky. This practice helps decrease the
automaticity of negative thinking. Chancing your thinking patterns
(cognitive restructuring) is a technique often used in cognitive-
behavioral therapy that involves identifying and challenging
distorted or unhelpful thoughts and replacing them with more
balanced and constructive ones. For instance, if you find yourself
thinking, "I always mess things up," you might reframe it to,
"Sometimes I make mistakes, but I often succeed as well." This shift
softens your self-view and opens you up to a more realistic and
forgiving perspective.

Building Resilience: The Fruit of a Compassionate Mind

The ultimate gift of transforming your inner dialogue is resilience.
When your self-talk is compassionate, setbacks become less about
failure and more about opportunities for growth. This doesn't mean
you won't feel disappointed or frustrated, but these feelings won't
knock you down as hard or keep you there as long. You'll be more
equipped to bounce back, learn from the experience, and move
forward. This resilience is crucial not just for facing personal challenges but also for navigating the complex, often harsh realities of
the world.

Transforming your inner dialogue from self-criticism to self-
compassion is like turning down the volume on a harsh, relentless

critic and tuning into a supportive, encouraging mentor. It's a shift that softens how you view yourself and fundamentally changes how you engage with the world. As you practice and strengthen this compassionate voice, you may find yourself not only more resilient in the face of life's challenges but also more open to the joys and opportunities life has to offer.

This chapter has taken us through understanding the roots of self-criticism, the transformative power of self-compassion, and practical techniques to cultivate a kinder inner dialogue. As we move forward, remember each small step in this practice is a leap toward building a stronger, more supportive relationship with yourself. In the next chapter, we will explore the practical everyday applications of self-love, turning the concepts and techniques discussed into tangible actions that can be incorporated into daily life. This transition marks a shift from understanding to action, from introspection to application, ensuring that the journey of self-love continues to be as enriching and transformative as possible.

Please refer to the "Journal Prompts" section at the end of the book and follow the prompts for Chapter 4.

CHAPTER FIVE

CULTIVATING INNER STRENGTH

Ever played one of those video games where your character has to go through various levels, gaining skills and strength along the way? Each challenge you overcome makes you stronger, more resilient, and somehow more graceful under pressure. Building inner strength in real life is a bit like leveling up in those games. It's about developing resilience, grit, and grace—qualities that don't just appear overnight but are honed through experiences and deliberate practice.

5.1 THE INNER STRENGTH FORMULA: RESILIENCE, GRIT, AND GRACE

Building Resilience: The Art of Bouncing Back

Resilience is the ability to bounce back from setbacks, roll with the punches, and come out standing. Think of it as your emotional shock absorber. Life, as you know, can throw some pretty wild curveballs. Building resilience means not just surviving these challenges but learning from them and growing into a stronger, more resilient version of yourself each time.

So, how do you develop this incredible resilience? It starts with your mindset. Viewing stress and hardship as natural, even beneficial parts of life can dramatically change how you respond to them. It's like changing your lens from one that only sees obstacles to one that spots opportunities. This positive adaptation involves recognizing that every hardship carries a seed of growth and learning. When you start to see challenges as catalysts for development, not as threats to your happiness or success, you build a kind of psychological resilience that powers you through life's ups and downs. To practice this, try reframing a recent challenge you faced. Instead of seeing it as a setback, look for the lessons it taught you and the opportunities it presented for growth. This simple exercise can help you start cultivating resilience in your daily life.

Cultivating Grit: The Power of Perseverance

Grit is that unyielding courage and determination that keeps you going, no matter what. It's about having long-term goals and the persistence to stick with them, even when the going gets tough. Grit is the stamina in your character; it's what helps you keep pushing forward, even when you feel like giving up.

But here's the thing about grit—it's not just about working hard. It's about working consistently toward something that deeply matters to you. It's passion married with perseverance. To build grit, start by defining what you're truly passionate about. What drives you? What big, audacious goal lights a fire in your belly? Once you have that vision clear, set small, achievable goals that lead you toward the larger one. This sustained effort over time not only moves you closer to your dreams but also builds your mental and emotional muscles, making you grittier with each step.

Embracing Grace: The Beauty of Forgiveness

Grace is perhaps the most overlooked yet vital component of inner strength. Grace is about handling yourself and others with compassion and forgiveness. It's the gentle art of letting go of grudges, forgiving yourself for your mistakes, and moving forward with wisdom and peace.

Developing grace starts with self-compassion. Be as kind to yourself in your failures as you are in your successes. Understand that being human means being imperfect, and that's okay. Extend this compassion outward, forgiving others not because they necessarily deserve it but because you deserve peace. Practicing forgiveness, much like resilience and grit, is a skill that strengthens with use. It smooths out the rough edges of your experiences, allowing you to heal from your wounds and face life with a softer, braver heart.

Interactive Element: Journaling for Growth

Start a resilience journal. Each day for one week, write down a challenge you faced and how you responded to it. Reflect on what you learned and how you could improve your response in the future. This simple practice tracks your progress and reinforces your growing resilience and grit. Over time, you'll see patterns and growth that will inspire and motivate you to keep pushing forward.

Cultivating inner strength through resilience, grit, and grace transforms how you face life's challenges. Instead of being knocked down by adversity, you'll learn to navigate it with wisdom, learning from each experience and growing into a stronger, more capable you. Remember, every challenge is an opportunity to level up in the game of life, and you've got what it takes to win.

5.2 OVERCOMING THE DOUBT MONSTER: STRATEGIES FOR RESILIENCE

Imagine your mind as a garden where thoughts grow like plants. Now, envision self-doubt as those stubborn weeds that sprout up no matter how often you try to get rid of them. They can be persistent and invasive; if left unchecked, they might overshadow your beautiful, flourishing plants. But here's the good news: just as gardeners develop strategies to manage weeds, you, too, can cultivate techniques to manage and overcome self-doubt, turning your mental garden into a place of resilience and growth.

One of the first steps in this gardening project is to get up close and personal with those weeds. It's about identifying the specific negative beliefs that fuel your self-doubt. Often, these beliefs are rooted in past experiences or messages from others that we've internalized without even realizing it. Maybe it's a voice that whispers you're not smart enough because you struggled in a particular class or a shadow that looms, telling you that you will never succeed because you've failed before. Recognizing these thoughts as the invasive weeds they are is crucial. Write them down, say them out loud, and stare them down. Understanding what you're dealing with gives you the power to challenge and change it, making you feel empowered and in control of your thoughts and beliefs.

Now, let's talk about pulling these weeds out. This is where challenging those negative beliefs comes into play. Suppose you have a recurring thought that you're not good at public speaking because of one awkward presentation. Challenge this by listing times you successfully communicated your ideas in other settings. Maybe you explained a game well at a family gathering or contributed a great idea during a team meeting. By recalling these moments, you're not just countering the negative belief but also reminding yourself of your capabilities, which can dilute the potency of self-doubt.

Setting achievable goals is like planting new, healthy plants in the cleared spaces of your garden. These goals should be specific, measurable, and realistic, providing a clear path forward and enabling you to mark progress. For instance, if you doubt your writing skills, set a goal to write a short story or a daily journal entry. As you meet these small goals, celebrate your successes—no matter how small. This could be as simple as treating yourself to your favorite snack or sharing your achievement with a friend. Each celebration is a sprinkle of water on your new plants, encouraging them to grow strong and vibrant.

Finally, no gardener tends their plot alone, and neither should you. Seeking support from trusted friends, family, or mentors can nourish your garden with new perspectives and encouragement. Just talking about your doubts can lessen their hold on you. These conversations can act like sunshine breaking through clouds, helping to clear the fog of doubt. Plus, these supporters can offer practical advice and reminders of your past successes when your own recall might be clouded by self-doubt.

Remember, overcoming self-doubt isn't about achieving a state of unwavering self-confidence overnight. It's about regular maintenance of your mental garden, pulling out weeds of negative belief, planting seeds of positive action, and nurturing them with recognition and support. This ongoing process builds a resilient mindset, empowering you to face life's challenges with a stronger, more confident self. So, grab your 'gardening tools'—your journal, your goals, your support network—and start tending to your garden with care. Each step you take is a step toward a lush, vibrant mind garden where self-doubt is managed and resilience blooms beautifully.

5.3 BUILDING A RESILIENT MINDSET: PRACTICES FOR EVERYDAY CHALLENGES

Think of building a resilient mindset as updating the operating system of your mind. It's about installing new habits that enhance your adaptability and optimism, ensuring you're equipped to handle whatever life throws your way. Every day, small but powerful practices can be integrated into your routine, gradually shifting how you perceive and react to challenges. It's like crafting a mental toolkit that makes you not just survive but thrive, no matter the weather.

Cultivating Daily Resilience through Mindfulness and Meditation

Let's kick off with mindfulness and meditation—two practices that are like the Swiss Army knives of mental wellness tools. Integrating mindfulness into your day isn't about sitting cross-legged for hours in silence. It's about becoming more aware of the present moment, whether you're eating, walking, or even having a conversation. This heightened awareness reduces automatic reactions to stress and fosters a more thoughtful approach to life's challenges. For instance, when you're fully present while eating, you savor each bite, making the meal more satisfying and enjoyable, which in turn can decrease stress eating.

Meditation, on the other hand, strengthens your ability to concentrate and remain calm. Starting with just five minutes a day can make a significant difference. During meditation, when you notice your mind wandering to the grocery list or an awkward email you need to send, gently bring it back to your breath or a meditation app's guiding words. This practice enhances your control over where your attention goes, which is incredibly powerful in high-stress situations where your instinct might be to panic or overreact.

Problem-Solving Skills: Turning Challenges into Opportunities

Now, on to developing problem-solving skills. Life loves to throw problems our way, and having a proactive approach means you see these problems as puzzles to solve rather than roadblocks in your path. Start small by tackling everyday issues with a can-do attitude. For example, if you find yourself running late for an appointment because of unexpected traffic, instead of spiraling into frustration, use the time to listen to a podcast or audiobook, turning a stressful situation into an opportunity for learning or relaxation.

Another aspect of honing your problem-solving skills involves planning for potential obstacles in advance. Before starting a new project or making a decision, take a few moments to think about what could go wrong and how you would handle it. This doesn't mean dwelling on the negative but preparing yourself to face challenges head-on. It's like putting on your mental armor, ready to battle whatever comes your way with grace and strategy.

The Role of Gratitude in Fostering Resilience

Cultivating gratitude is another cornerstone of building a resilient mindset. It's easy to focus on what's going wrong in our lives, but shifting the focus to what's going right can dramatically alter our perspective. Make it a habit to jot down three things you're grateful for each day. These could be as simple as a delicious cup of coffee, a call from a friend, or the feeling of sunshine on your face. This practice trains your brain to notice and appreciate the positive, which can buffer against the negative effects of stress.

Gratitude doesn't just make you feel better; it also strengthens your relationships. When you express appreciation to others, it deepens your connection with them, creating a supportive network that's crucial for resilience. It's like weaving a safety net of positive interactions and support, ensuring that when things get tough, you're not alone.

Staying Grounded in the Present: The Antidote to Stress

Lastly, focusing on the present can be incredibly powerful in reducing stress. It's about taking life one step at a time. When over-whelmed, remind yourself of where you are right now. Feel your feet on the ground, listen to the sounds around you, and take a deep breath. This simple act of grounding can help dissolve the mountain of anxiety into manageable hills, making each step forward less daunting.

Each of these practices—mindfulness, meditation, proactive prob-lem-solving, gratitude, and staying present—are tools that, when used daily, can profoundly enhance resilience. They don't require massive lifestyle changes. Still, they can be seamlessly integrated into your daily routine, offering a steady foundation of strength and adaptability.

As we close this chapter on building a resilient mindset, remember that each practice is a thread in the larger tapestry of your life. Together, they form a resilient, vibrant picture, full of color and strength, ready to face whatever challenges come next. In the following chapter, we'll explore how nurturing your emotional and mental well-being is not just beneficial but essential for a balanced life, ensuring that the foundation we've built in resilience is complemented by deep, sustaining care for your inner world.

Please refer to the "Journal Prompts" section at the end of the book and follow the prompts for Chapter 5.

CHAPTER SIX

NURTURING YOUR EMOTIONAL AND MENTAL WELL-BEING

I magine your emotions are like a garden. Now, every gardener knows that a flourishing garden isn't just about planting seeds and hoping for the best; it's about regular nurturing, understanding the soil, and sometimes sitting back and enjoying the blooming flowers. Similarly, taking care of your emotional and mental well-being isn't just a one-off task—it's an ongoing process that involves tuning in to your inner world, understanding your emotional landscape, and cultivating practices that keep you mentally and emotionally balanced. Today, let's roll up our sleeves and get our hands a little dirty in the rich soil of our emotions, shall we?

6.1 EMOTIONAL GARDENING: TENDING TO YOUR FEELINGS

Recognizing and Validating Your Emotional Flora

The first step to effective emotional gardening is not just recognizing but empowering yourself to validate your feelings. Just like a gardener needs to recognize the signs of under-watering or overexposure to the sun, you must acknowledge and validate whatever emotions crop up. It's easy to dismiss feelings like sadness or anxiety as mere nuisances. However, just like every weed has a way of telling the gardener about the health of the garden, every emotion you experience has something important to convey about your emotional and mental state. By validating these emotions, you take the reins of your emotional well-being, steering it toward a healthier state.

Consider your emotions as indicators in your garden of well-being. When you experience joy, it's like seeing your plants thrive—signaling that the conditions are favorable. On the other hand, feelings of discomfort or distress might indicate that something in your environment needs to be adjusted, much like a plant showing signs of wilt or stress due to unsuitable soil or inadequate sunlight. By acknowledging these emotions without judgment, you engage in a nurturing process, tending to your needs with the same care a gardener would give to their garden. This dialogue with yourself is healing and enlightening, as it helps you understand the underlying needs your emotions are pointing to.

Cultivating Through Journaling and Expressive Arts

Now, how do you effectively process these emotions? One way is through journaling and engaging in expressive arts. These activities allow you to articulate feelings that might be hard to express verbally and provide a comforting space for your emotions to be understood. Think of journaling as planting seeds of awareness; as you write, you're sowing seeds that will eventually grow into a deeper understanding of your emotional self. The act of transferring thoughts onto paper can be incredibly therapeutic. It's a way to externalize what's internal, which can make your feelings more manageable and less intimidating.

Expressive arts, whether it's painting, music, or dance, can also be a powerful tool for emotional expression. These creative outlets provide a non-verbal language for emotions that are too complex or overwhelming to articulate. For example, using colors in a painting can express feelings you might not have words for. This process is not just about creating art; it's about letting your emotions flow through you and manifest in a form that can be seen, touched, or heard, which can be incredibly validating and cathartic.

Reflective Time in Your Emotional Garden

Consider self-reflection as a dedicated time to walk through your emotional garden, taking stock of its growth and needs. It's essential to slow down and allocate time for this process, much like a gardener methodically surveys their garden to understand what needs nurturing or pruning. In our fast-paced world, it's easy to neglect this vital practice, but just as a garden requires regular attention to thrive, so do our emotional landscapes.

Taking time for self-reflection allows us to step back from the daily rush and examine our feelings and reactions. This pause is not just a break but a crucial intervention that helps us make sense of our experiences, identify what enriches us, and recognize elements that may be stifling our growth. By slowing down and reflecting, we can better understand our emotional responses and the triggers that influence them, leading to more informed decisions about how to cultivate a healthier mental and emotional state.

This practice helps you connect the dots between what you're feeling and why you're feeling it. It's about asking yourself questions like, "What's really bothering me?" or "Why did that comment affect me so deeply?" This kind of introspection can help you understand the root causes of your emotional responses, much like a gardener understanding why certain plants aren't thriving.

Self-reflection can be structured, like setting aside a few minutes each evening to reflect on the day's emotional highs and lows, or it can be more spontaneous, like assessing your feelings during a particularly stressful situation. The key is consistency and honesty. The more regularly you engage in this practice, the deeper your understanding of your emotional self becomes, leading to more effective emotional regulation.

Cultivating Positive Emotions

Just as gardeners cultivate more of the flowers they love, you can cultivate more of the emotions that bring joy and satisfaction. Engaging in activities that you know bring you happiness is like watering the plants you want to thrive.

Imagine your week is like a garden plot, where every task you have is a shrub that takes up space and requires attention. Finding time for things that bring you joy—like reading, walking, or catching up with friends—is like planting your favorite flowers among these shrubs. It might seem tricky at first, with the garden already so full, but here's how you can make room for those blooms:

1. **Mark Your Calendar:** Think of these joyful activities as essential appointments. Write them down in your planner just like you would a work meeting. Whether it's a quick walk or a few minutes with a book before bed, seeing it scheduled will help you make it happen.
2. **Mix It Into Your Day:** Find ways to blend your favorite things into your activities. You can listen to your favorite tunes or a new podcast while commuting or doing dishes. If nature calms you, try taking a different route to work that lets you walk through a park.
3. **Start Small:** If your days are packed, begin with just five or

ten minutes of something enjoyable. Once you get used to that little break, you might find it easier to extend it.

4. **Let Technology Help:** Set reminders on your phone to take a quick break or use apps that encourage you to pause and relax. These little prompts can be your nudge to take a step back and breathe.

5. **Learn to Say No:** Look at your to-do list and ask yourself: Do I really need to do all of this? Maybe some tasks can wait, or perhaps someone else can help. Dropping a less necessary chore can free up some time for your happiness.

6. **Think About What Matters Most:** Every now and then, sit down and think about what makes you happiest. Is your schedule reflecting these priorities? If not, it might be time for some changes so your days align more with your joys and less with just duties.

By prioritizing these joy-filled moments as essentials, not extras, you'll begin to realize their transformative power. Even the fullest garden can accommodate a few favorite flowers. And just like that, your week won't be solely about completing tasks but also about savoring moments that make life brighter and more fulfilling.

This cultivation of positive emotions is essential because it doesn't just add joy to your life; it also creates a buffer against negative emotions. When you have a reserve of positive emotions, you are better equipped to handle life's inevitable challenges. It's like a gardener who not only plants new flowers but also nurtures the soil, making it rich and robust enough to support all kinds of plants during the various seasons of growth.

In nurturing your emotional and mental well-being, remember that it's not about achieving a state of perpetual happiness or a garden without weeds—it's about developing the tools and practices that allow you to manage and make the most of all your emotional experiences. Just as a well-tended garden brings joy to the gardener and beauty to the world, a well-nurtured emotional life enriches your existence and radiates outward, positively affecting those around you. Now, let's carry these tools and insights forward as we continue to explore deeper into the practices that can transform our relationship with our minds and emotions, fostering a resilient, joyful, and balanced life.

6.2 MINDFULNESS IN ACTION: TECHNIQUES FOR PEACE

Imagine you're in the middle of a hectic day, your phone is buzzing, your inbox is overflowing, and you've got back-to-back meetings that probably should have been emails. Now, picture taking a moment amid that chaos to close your eyes, take a deep breath, and just be present. That, right there, is mindfulness in action, a simple yet profoundly effective tool for navigating the whirlwinds of daily life with a bit more grace and a lot less stress.

Mindfulness, put simply, is the practice of paying full attention to the present moment without judgment. It's about noticing your experiences, thoughts, and feelings without trying to change them. Think of it as tuning into a radio station—Mindfulness FM—where the only broadcast is what's happening right here, right now. This practice enhances your awareness of the present, which can dramatically reduce stress and anxiety. Why? Because when you're fully engaged with the present, you're not fretting about past mistakes or worrying about future problems. You're too busy noticing the now, and it's hard to stress about a meeting next week when you're genuinely absorbed in the sensations of your current environment.

Integrating mindfulness into your daily routine can be surprisingly easy and does not require any special equipment—just a bit of time and intention. One effective exercise is the "Mindful Pause." All you need to do is set a timer on your phone to remind you periodically throughout the day to take a brief pause. During this pause, engage all your senses to fully experience the moment. What do you see? Perhaps light filtering through a window or the movement of people around you. What do you hear? Maybe the distant sound of traffic or the hum of your computer. What do you feel? The chair beneath you, the air on your skin? This practice doesn't need to take long—just a minute or two every hour can profoundly impact your ability to manage stress and stay grounded.

Another simple yet effective mindfulness technique is the "Single-Task Challenge." This involves choosing an activity you'd normally do on autopilot—like brushing your teeth or making coffee—and focusing all your attention on the task. Notice every aspect of the activity:

For example, let's dive deeper into the experience of enjoying a warm cup of coffee:

Imagine it's early morning, and the first thing you do is head to the kitchen. You grab the bag of coffee beans—maybe they're your favorite roast that's a bit nutty and sweet. You hear the beans pour into the grinder, and as they grind, the aroma begins to fill the air. It's rich and inviting, a smell that seems to wrap around you like a warm blanket.

Now, you scoop the grounds into your coffee maker and start the brew. The sound of the coffee dripping is steady and comforting, a familiar part of your routine. When it's ready, you pour the steaming coffee into your mug, feeling the warmth spread through the ceramic to your hands. It's soothing, almost like holding a little piece of the morning sun.

As you take that first sip, the warmth flows through you. The flavor is just right, a perfect balance of bitterness and the natural sweet-ness of the beans. It's a moment to pause, savor, and truly wake up your body and your senses.

This daily ritual is more than just about drinking coffee; it's a sensory journey that begins your day on a note of mindfulness and pleasure, grounding you for what's ahead.

This practice enhances your sensory experiences and trains your brain to focus more effectively, reducing the scatterbrained feeling that often accompanies multitasking.

Mindfulness also encourages a non-judgmental attitude toward yourself and your experiences. It's about observing your thoughts and feelings without labeling them as good or bad. This attitude can be particularly liberating when dealing with negative emotions. Instead of getting caught up in self-criticism for feeling anxious or upset, mindfulness allows you to acknowledge your feelings with compassion and understanding. This acceptance can be incredibly calming, as it prevents you from spiraling into further stress or anxiety over your initial emotional response. It's like giving yourself permission to feel whatever you're feeling, which, paradoxically, often leads to a greater sense of peace.

The benefits of regular mindfulness practice are not just psychological; they're also physical. Research has shown that consistent mindfulness exercises can change brain structure and function. Areas of the brain associated with attention and sensory processing become more developed. At the same time, regions linked to stress and anxiety may show reduced activity. These changes can enhance your overall well-being, making you more resilient to stress and more focused and effective in your daily life.

Incorporating mindfulness into your routine doesn't require drastic changes. It starts with small moments, little pauses throughout your day, where you tune into the present and tune out the noise. Over time, these moments build up, creating a profound shift in how you experience your life. They transform fleeting days filled with forgettable tasks into a series of vivid, lived moments, each one appreciated and fully experienced. So, why not give it a try?

Start small, perhaps with the Mindful Pause or the Single-Task Challenge, and watch as the practice of mindfulness begins to transform not just the minutes of your day but the very quality of your life.

6.3 STRESS-BUSTING STRATEGIES: FROM OVERWHELMED TO CALM

Have you ever felt like your day is a string of emails, notifications, and deadlines that just won't quit? And just when you think you can catch a breath, something else pops up. Stress, that unwelcome guest, can throw a wrench in our daily serenity. But here's the scoop: becoming adept at managing stress isn't just about dodging these curveballs; it's about developing a toolkit that helps you deal with them effectively when they inevitably come your way.

Unraveling Your Stress Threads

First things first, identifying what triggers your stress is crucial. It's like being a detective in your own life: which events, situations, or people make your heart race or your temper flare? Sometimes, it's obvious, like a big presentation at work. Other times, it might be subtler, like a cluttered home environment that quietly frays your nerves. Understanding these triggers is the first step in crafting a strategy that's tailored to keep your stress levels in check. Once you know your triggers, you can start to work on responses that help keep your cool. For instance, if time pressure stresses you out, maybe start breaking tasks into smaller, manageable chunks and setting realistic deadlines.

Quick-Fix Stress Busters

Now, for immediate stress relief, there are a few techniques that can feel almost like magic. Let's start with deep breathing exercises. It sounds so simple, yet it's incredibly powerful. By focusing on taking slow, deep breaths, you activate your body's natural relaxation response. This helps decrease your heart rate and blood pressure, bringing a calm over your body that can fend off the tidal wave of stress hormones like cortisol. Then, there's progressive muscle relaxation, which involves tensing and relaxing different muscle groups in your body.

Here's how you might experience it:

You might start at your feet, tightening the muscles as much as you can—imagine you're trying to curl your toes. Hold that tension, really feel it build, and then suddenly let it go. Notice the rush of relief and relaxation that follows. It's like releasing a clenched fist, feeling the muscles loosen and soften.

Next, you move up to your calves, then your thighs, repeating the process. As you work your way up your body, from your stomach to your chest, and then to your arms and shoulders, you're paying close attention to each area. It's a way to discover where you might be holding stress without even realizing it.

This method doesn't just ease the physical tension; it also encourages a deep connection between mind and body. You become more aware of where stress accumulates in your body and learn to consciously relax those areas. It's like conducting a thorough scan and repair job on your body, which can leave you feeling more relaxed and mentally clear.

Guided imagery is another fantastic tool. It involves visualizing a peaceful scene, such as a quiet beach or a serene forest. By immersing yourself in these calming mental images, you can shift your focus away from the stressors, giving your mind and body a mini-vacation. You can easily find guided imagery sessions online or through various apps, making this stress-relief method accessible at home, in the office, or even commuting.

Long-Term Strategies for a Stress-Less Lifestyle

While immediate techniques are great for acute stress, long-term stress management usually calls for lifestyle changes. Regular physical activity is a cornerstone here. Whether it's yoga, jogging, or dancing, moving your body helps reduce stress and boosts your endorphins, those feel-good hormones that are natural stress fighters.

Then, there's the role of a balanced diet and adequate sleep, which are often underestimated. Eating a balanced diet fuels your body with the nutrients necessary to combat stress, while enough sleep ensures you have the energy to face the day's challenges. Together, these habits form a foundation that not only helps you manage stress but also enhances your overall well-being.

Cultivating Your Support Garden

Finally, never underestimate the power of a strong support network. Connecting with friends, family, or even colleagues who understand and support you can make a world of difference. Just knowing you're not alone in your struggles can reduce stress. For those times when stress feels too heavy, reaching out to a professional, like a therapist, life coach, or counselor, can provide the tools and perspective needed to manage stress effectively. It's like having a guide in the complex journey of managing your stress— someone who can offer insights and strategies that are tailored just for you.

As we wrap this chapter, remember that managing stress is less about avoiding challenges and more about equipping yourself with the tools to tackle them head-on. Whether it's identifying your triggers, employing quick relaxation techniques, making lifestyle adjustments, or leaning on your support network, each strategy you employ weaves a stronger safety net, enabling you to handle stress with more grace and resilience. As you continue to build and refine your stress-management toolkit, let these strategies empower you to transform your relationship with stress, turning what once overwhelmed you into something you can manage and master.

In the next chapter, we will explore the intricate relationship between self-love and your interactions with others, delving into how nurturing self-love can enhance and transform your personal relationships. The journey continues to unfold, with each step offering new insights and tools for living a more balanced and fulfilling life.

Please refer to the "Journal Prompts" section at the end of the book and follow the prompts for Chapter 6.

CHAPTER SEVEN
SELF-CARE AS A FOUNDATION

Ah, self-care. You've probably seen it hashtagged on a million Instagram posts, usually accompanying a picture of someone in a face mask, holding a glass of wine in a bubble bath. But let's strip away the froth and get real for a moment. Self-care isn't just about those indulgent moments (as delightful as they are); it's about crafting a lifestyle that supports and sustains you, body and soul. It's about tuning into your needs and ensuring you're not just surviving but thriving. Let's dive deeper into what self-care truly means and how you can transform it from a luxury into a cornerstone of your daily life, a practice that can truly change your life for the better.

7.1 REDEFINING SELF-CARE: BEYOND THE BUBBLE BATH

So, what's the real scoop on self-care? It's simple yet profound: self-care is any activity we do deliberately to care for our mental, emotional, and physical health. Sounds straightforward, right? Yet, it's astonishing how often these essential activities get bumped off our to-do lists. We tend to treat self-care as a luxury, reserved for when we have spare time—time that, let's be honest, rarely comes. But self-care isn't a luxury. It's essential, and it's time we start treating it that way.

Self-care is holistic. It's not just about keeping your body fit or your skin glowing; it's about nurturing your whole self. This includes your physical health, sure, but also your mental well-being, your emotional resilience, and, yes, even your spiritual fulfillment. It's about feeding every part of yourself that needs attention. Sometimes, that might mean hitting the gym or booking a spa day, but other times, it might be as simple as seeking out a heartfelt conversation with a friend or taking a quiet moment to meditate or pray.

Incorporating self-care into your daily life isn't about carving out massive chunks of your day; it's about recognizing the value of small, consistent practices. It's understanding that every little bit counts and that these small moments of care can profoundly impact your overall well-being. It's about changing the narrative from self-care as an indulgence to self-care as a fundamental practice for long-term health and happiness. And the best part? These practices are simple, accessible, and can be seamlessly integrated into your busy life, giving you the power to take control of your well-being.

Here's where it gets really personal. Self-care isn't one-size-fits-all. What works wonders for one person might not work for you. The key is to understand and embrace your unique needs and circumstances. This might mean adjusting your self-care practices to fit a hectic schedule or finding activities that address specific health concerns or emotional states. It's about listening—really listening—to your body, your mind, and your heart and responding with kindness and care.

Crafting Your Personal Self-Care Plan

Think about what truly replenishes you. Is it physical activity? Quiet reflection? Creative expression? Social interaction? Start by making a list of activities under each of these categories. Then, take a moment each day to engage in at least one activity from your list. It doesn't have to be for long—even a few minutes can make a difference. This simple practice can help you build a self-care routine that fits seamlessly into your life, ensuring that you're nurturing every part of yourself.

In redefining self-care, we uncover its true essence: a practice not of indulgence but of necessity. It's a commitment to treating yourself with the same kindness and attention that you offer to others. It's a recognition that maintaining your health and happiness is not just beneficial but essential for a whole and fulfilling life. As we continue to explore the depths and breadths of self-care, remember that this journey is deeply personal and immensely rewarding. Here's to making self-care a foundational stone in the beautiful architecture of your life, one small, deliberate step at a time.

7.2 CUSTOMIZABLE SELF-CARE: YOUR ROUTINE, YOUR RULES

If self-care were a recipe, think of it not as a strict baking formula but more like a freestyle smoothie where you toss in ingredients that suit your taste and nourish your body uniquely. This approach underscores a crucial idea: self-care is deeply personal, and what stirs tranquility in one person might not even stir a spoon for another. It's about finding what resonates with your soul, fits into your schedule, and meets your needs at different phases of your life. Let's peel back the layers on how you can craft a self-care routine that's as unique as you are.

Now, imagine your life as a canvas and self-care as the palette of colors you choose to paint with. Some days, you might go for bold, vibrant shades—activities that energize and invigorate you. On other days, you might opt for soft pastels—soothing practices that help calm and restore you. The beauty lies in your ability to choose and change your palette as needed. For instance, while a five-mile run might be perfect for times when you're overflowing with energy, a quiet evening with a book might better suit a day when you're drained. Experimenting with different activities allows you to discover what you enjoy and what truly benefits you in varying life contexts.

This experimentation is not about haphazardly jumping from one activity to another but about tuning in to your body and mind's responses. Suppose you try yoga and notice that you feel more grounded and less reactive to stress on days you practice. That's valuable feedback. Or maybe you find that journaling before bed clears your mind and aids in better sleep. These insights help you craft a self-care routine that isn't just effective but sustainable because it's tailored to your natural rhythms and life realities.

Regular reflection on your self-care practices is like doing periodic check-ins at a favorite retreat spot. It's about asking, "Is this still serving me?" or "What do I need more or less of?" Life is ever-changing—new challenges and transitions can shift your self-care needs. Regular reflection helps you adjust your practices to continue serving you well.

Adapting self-care routines to fit different schedules and energy levels is crucial, especially in our fast-paced world. It's about being realistic—acknowledging that while a weekend might allow for a long nature hike, a busy workday might only permit a few minutes of deep breathing between meetings. It's recognizing that self-care doesn't have to be time-consuming to be effective; it's about making the most of your pockets of time. For instance, integrating a five-minute mindfulness practice right before you start your day can be incredibly beneficial if you have a hectic morning routine. For someone else, using lunch breaks for a brisk walk or a quiet moment away from the desk might be the perfect recharge.

Remember, crafting your personalized self-care plan is not about rigidly sticking to a prescribed set of activities. It's about fluidity and flexibility—allowing yourself to adapt and evolve your practices as your life changes. It's about embracing the freedom to define what care means for you and using that understanding to nurture yourself in the most genuine way possible. So, let's start, mix and match, try new things, keep what works, and gently set aside what doesn't, crafting a self-care routine that truly reflects and supports who you are and aspire to be.

7.3 SELF-CARE ON THE GO: QUICK FIXES FOR BUSY LIVES

Let's face it, the modern mantra seems to be "so much to do, so little time." In the whirlwind of day-to-day tasks, self-care can often feel like a luxury cruise when you barely have time for a quick paddle in the pool. But here's the kicker: self-care doesn't have to be time-consuming or lavish. It's possible to weave it seamlessly into the fabric of your dizzyingly busy life, turning fleeting moments into oases of calm and rejuvenation.

The notion that self-care must be a grand gesture is not only overwhelming but downright impractical. Think of self-care as mini-pauses or "micro-luxe" moments that you can sprinkle throughout your day without disrupting your schedule. These aren't just stop-gaps; they're powerful bursts of refreshment that can significantly uplift your mood and energy levels.

One of the simplest yet most profound techniques is mindful breathing. This can be done anywhere, anytime. Whether you're in a long queue, stuck in traffic, or between meetings, taking a few deep, intentional breaths can center your thoughts and lower stress levels. Imagine each breath washing over you like a gentle wave, clearing away tension and refreshing your mind. It's a pocket-sized retreat you can escape to without ever leaving your spot.

Gratitude journaling is another gem in the treasure chest of quick self-care practices. You don't need to compose lengthy entries; just jotting down one or two things you're grateful for each day can shift your perspective from what's lacking to what's abundant. This practice can be especially uplifting during those days that feel like a relentless grind. By focusing on the positives, however small, you cultivate a mindset that can transform ordinary moments into extraordinary ones. Keep a small notebook handy, or use a notes app to capture these gratitude nuggets. Over time, this habit enhances your mood and fortifies your emotional resilience, making you more content and optimistic.

Walking breaks are yet another strategy that marries simplicity with efficacy. Instead of scrolling through your phone during a break, why not take a brisk walk around the block or even just around your office? This isn't just about physical activity; it's about giving your mind a fresh scene and your body a chance to stretch and breathe. If you're working from home, a brief walk in your garden or down your street can act as a perfect reset button, clearing your mental cache and boosting creativity.

However, despite knowing these strategies, many of us still stumble over barriers like guilt, lack of time, or external pressures. Overcoming these requires a shift in mindset. First, eradicate the guilt associated with taking time for yourself by redefining these moments as necessities rather than indulgences. Just as you wouldn't feel guilty for charging your phone, don't feel guilty for recharging your own batteries. Regarding time constraints, remember that self-care doesn't need to be time-consuming. It's about quality, not quantity. Integrating small acts of care throughout your day can be more beneficial than a rare, extended session.

External pressures can also be daunting. The world won't stop if you take a few minutes for yourself, but your world may improve significantly if you do. Set boundaries where necessary and communicate openly about your need for brief self-care breaks. Most will respect your commitment to maintaining your well-being; you might even inspire others to follow suit.

In navigating through the bustling corridors of your daily routines, remember that self-care is not a destination but a method of travel. It's about making the journey smoother, more enjoyable, and, yes, more sustainable. As you continue to explore and integrate these quick, effective self-care practices into your life, you'll likely find that they not only enhance your days but fundamentally enrich your overall well-being.

Please refer to the "Journal Prompts" section at the end of the book and follow the prompts for Chapter 7.

MAKE A DIFFERENCE WITH YOUR REVIEW
UNLOCK THE POWER OF GENEROSITY

"Kindness is the language which the deaf can hear, and the blind can see."

— MARK TWAIN

Did you know people who give selflessly often lead happier, more fulfilling lives? It's true! They say the best things in life aren't things at all but the actions we take to make the world a better place. And here's where you come in.

Ever thought about how a simple act of kindness could change someone's life? Well, that's precisely what your book review could do!

Imagine a person just like you, maybe how you were a few years ago. Someone eager to grow and learn but still trying to figure out where to start. That person is out there, and they need your help to discover **The Self-Love Guide: Master Techniques to Overcome Low Self-Esteem, Quiet Self-Doubt, and Crush Negative Self-Talk. Unlock Your Full Potential and Embark on Your Journey Toward Your Best You.**

Here at Willow.Cedar.Sage Collective, everything we do is about spreading self-love and empowerment. We rely on help from kind souls like you to reach everyone who needs this message.

Most folks do judge a book by its cover—and its reviews! So, here's my big ask on behalf of a future self-lover you haven't met yet:

Please leave this book a review.

It won't cost you a dime, just a minute of your time, but your words could make a massive difference. Your review could help:

- One more individual find self-acceptance.
- One more dreamer chase their dreams.
- One more leader inspire their team.
- One more soul heal and grow.
- One more story of transformation be told.

Ready to share some kindness? It's super easy! Just scan this QR code to leave your review:

If helping someone anonymously excites you, you're definitely one of us! Welcome to the club.

I'm thrilled to help you on your journey to self-love, equipping you with all the strategies, insights, and actions you need. You'll love what's coming next.

Thank you from the bottom of my heart. Let's continue our journey together.

- Your biggest fan, the Willow.Cedar.Sage Collective

PS - Remember, when you offer something valuable, you become invaluable. If this book could help another soul, why not share it? Pass it on and spread the love!

CHAPTER EIGHT

OVERCOMING EXTERNAL CHALLENGES

E ver felt like you're on a rollercoaster that you didn't even choose to ride? That's often what diving into the world of social media can feel like. One minute, you're laughing at a clever meme, and the next, you're three years deep into a stranger's vacation photos, feeling like your own life can't measure up. With its glittering promises of connection and inspiration, social media also brings a hefty dose of self-doubt and pressure. So, how do you keep from drowning in the digital sea? Let's navigate these waters together, finding ways to harness these powerful tools without letting them steer your sense of self off course.

8.1 NAVIGATING SOCIAL MEDIA WITHOUT LOSING YOURSELF

Social media isn't just a way to pass the time; it's become a significant landscape where perceptions are formed and norms are challenged. But as much as it connects and uplifts, it can also distort and disrupt our self-esteem and self-perception. The trick isn't to shun these platforms but to engage with them more mindfully.

Imagine social media like a big party. You can let the loud, bois-terous conversations drown out your thoughts or seek meaningful exchanges that enrich and inspire you.

Setting Boundaries: Your Time, Your Rules

First, setting time limits on your social media use isn't about depriving yourself—it's about ensuring you don't slip into the vortex of endless scrolling. Much like deciding beforehand how many cookies you'll eat from the jar (because, let's be honest, left unchecked, we'd eat them all), decide how much time you can real-istically spend on these platforms without it affecting your mood or productivity. Tools that track your usage can be handy here. They're like fitness trackers but for your digital consumption, providing insights into your habits and helping you stick to your goals.

Curating Your Feed: A Diet for Your Mind

Curating your feed is crucial because, much like you are what you eat, you also become what you consume online. Unfollow accounts that trigger negative feelings or comparisons, and start following ones that motivate and uplift you. It's like tidying up your room; the more organized and positive it is, the better you feel spending time there. This doesn't mean you only follow accounts that show a never-ending reel of positivity—authenticity is key. It's about ensuring the content you consume adds value to your day and aligns with the kind of digital environment you want to cultivate.

The Role of Critical Consumption

Being a critical consumer on social media means not taking every-thing you see at face value. Just because something looks picture-perfect doesn't mean it's real. Most social media content is curated and edited—it's a highlight reel, not the behind-the-scenes. Keeping this in mind helps you maintain perspective, preventing you from falling into the trap of comparing your unfiltered life to someone else's filtered presentation. It's like watching a magic show; enjoy the spectacle, but remember, it's a performance, not real life.

Digital Detoxes: Reconnecting with the World

Finally, let's talk about the importance of digital detoxes. These are periods when you consciously decide to step away from digital devices. It's not about isolation but about reconnecting with yourself and the world around you. During a digital detox, engage in activities that you might have neglected—read that book that's been gathering dust on your shelf, go for a long walk, or have a face-to-face conversation with a friend. These detox periods can recharge your mental batteries and give you fresh perspectives, enriching your life both online and offline when you return.

Navigating social media mindfully allows you to reclaim control over your digital interactions. It ensures that social media remains a tool for connection and inspiration rather than a source of stress or insecurity. So, next time you log in, remember these strategies. They're not just guidelines but empowering practices that allow you to engage with social media on your own terms, making it a positive addition to your life rather than a detractor.

8.2 SAYING NO: THE POWER OF BOUNDARIES

Let's face it, saying "no" can sometimes feel like trying to swat a fly with a string of spaghetti—awkward, uncomfortable, and with a high chance of making a mess. Yet, setting boundaries is less about pushing people away and more about drawing a personal line in the sand that defines where you end and others begin. It's about protecting your time, energy, and emotional well-being from being drained by demands that don't align with your values or needs.

Imagine boundaries as the personal rules or guidelines you establish for yourself and others. They help you respect and take care of yourself, and they're essential for maintaining a healthy relationship with others and with yourself.

Now, identifying your personal limits can sometimes feel like trying to read a map in the dark. It requires a deep dive into understanding what makes you tick, what drains you, and what helps you flourish. Start by reflecting on past experiences where you felt overwhelmed, resentful, or depleted. These feelings are often indicators that your boundaries were either being tested or outright ignored. Once you have a clearer picture, articulate these limits to yourself. It might be something like, "I need to have one day each week where I don't make any social plans," or "I can't take work calls after six p.m." Remember, these aren't just whims; they are necessary measures to keep your well-being in check.

Communicating these boundaries can be as tricky as walking a tightrope, especially if you fear the potential backlash. Whether it's the worry about a friend's reaction to declining an invitation or the anxiety about a boss's response to a request for less overtime, the fear of conflict or rejection is real and palpable. However, clear and honest communication is the thread that can balance these fears. Approach these conversations with clarity and kindness—state what you need, why you need it, and how it's beneficial not just for you but for your relationship or job. For instance, telling a friend, "I value our time together, but I need to spend this weekend recharging by myself," prioritizes your mental health while also affirming your appreciation for the friendship.

The beauty of setting and respecting boundaries is that it doesn't just liberate you; it can transform your relationships. When you clearly communicate your needs, you invite others to understand and respect your perspective, paving the way for a relationship built on mutual respect and understanding. This clarity prevents resentments from building up, keeping interactions honest and transparent. Think about it: when both parties respect each other's boundaries, the relationship naturally becomes more supportive and less about guessing games or silent grievances.

Moreover, the act of setting boundaries is profoundly tied to self-respect and self-love. Each time you advocate for your needs, you send a powerful message to yourself and others that your feelings, time, and overall well-being are valuable. This not only boosts your self-esteem but also deepens your relationship with yourself. You become more in tune with what you truly need and less likely to compromise on the essentials. As these boundaries become more ingrained in your daily interactions, you'll find that you are protecting your energy and opening up more space to grow, create, and let in joy and peace—on your own terms.

8.3 DEALING WITH TOXIC RELATIONSHIPS: PROTECTING YOUR PEACE

Let's talk about something a bit heavy but incredibly important—dealing with toxic relationships. You know those relationships that drain your energy faster than a smartphone battery? They can make you doubt your worth, cloud your happiness, and sometimes leave scars on your self-esteem. Recognizing and stepping away from such toxic connections isn't just about saving yourself from drama; it's about preserving your peace and nurturing your self-love.

First things first, identifying a toxic relationship can be tricky. It's not always about the big arguments or glaring betrayals. Sometimes, it's the subtle things—a constant undercurrent of criticism, the persistent disregard for your boundaries, or a perennial feeling of being undervalued. These relationships often leave you feeling worse off like you're a plant trying to thrive in toxic soil. The effects on your self-worth can be profound. You might start questioning your value, second-guessing your decisions, and feeling smaller and less significant. It's a gradual erosion of self-love that can leave you feeling depleted and lost.

Now, how do you handle these toxic ties? It starts with recognizing the signs. Pay attention to how you feel before and after interacting with someone. Are you often left feeling drained, criticized, or unsupported? Does the relationship feel like a one-way street, where your needs and feelings are consistently sidelined? These are red flags waving at you, telling you that something's off. Once you've identified a toxic relationship, the next step is creating distance. This isn't about ghosting someone or an explosive confrontation. It's about gradually pulling back—spending less time with the person, not sharing as much personal information, and setting firm boundaries about what you will and will not tolerate.

Self-compassion is your ally. Remind yourself that stepping back isn't a sign of weakness or failure—it's a profound act of self-care. Be gentle with yourself during this process. It's okay to feel sad, guilty, or conflicted. These are normal emotions when you're distancing yourself from someone, especially if you've shared good times in the past. Allow yourself to grieve the loss of what the relationship could have been, but also remind yourself of why you're making this choice. You're choosing to prioritize your well-being, your peace, and your right to be treated with respect and kindness.

Seeking support plays a crucial role in this process. Talk to friends or family members who understand and support your decision. Sometimes, just voicing your feelings and experiences can be incredibly validating and healing. If the relationship has left deeper wounds, or if you're finding it difficult to navigate the detachment process, consider seeking help from a professional—a counselor, life coach, or therapist. These experts can offer you tools and strategies to heal from the impact of toxic relationships and can guide you in rebuilding your self-love and confidence.

Healing from toxic relationships is like rehabilitating a garden after it's been exposed to harmful chemicals. It takes time, care, and a lot of nurturing. Start by planting new seeds of self-appreciation. Engage in activities that reinforce your worth and bring you joy. Surround yourself with people who uplift you and reflect the love and respect you deserve. Over time, you'll see new growth—signs of recovery and renewal. Your self-esteem will begin to bloom again, stronger and more vibrant, rooted in a renewed sense of self-love and peace.

Navigating through and healing from toxic relationships is a crucial step in protecting not just your peace but also your ability to flourish and thrive. It's about cleaning the soil of your life so that you can grow unimpeded by negativity and doubt. As we wrap up this chapter, remember the importance of recognizing, distancing, and healing from these harmful connections. Each step away from toxicity is a step toward a healthier, happier you, paving the way for truly nourishing and fulfilling relationships.

As we close this chapter on overcoming external challenges, we move forward with the tools and confidence to protect our peace and cultivate environments that support our growth and happiness. Let's carry these insights into the next chapter, where we will explore the transformative power of self-love in action, turning the lessons we've learned into daily practices that enrich our lives.

Please refer to the "Journal Prompts" section at the end of the book and follow the prompts for Chapter 8.

CHAPTER NINE

TRANSFORMING RELATIONSHIPS WITH SELF-LOVE

E ver caught yourself singing passionately into a shampoo bottle, completely mesmerized by your reflection in the foggy mirror? There's something magical about those unguarded moments when you're your own audience. These instances, silly as they may seem, hint at a profound truth: the relationship you have with yourself sets the tone for every other relationship in your life. This chapter isn't just about loving yourself; it's about discovering how this deep, personal connection can transform every interaction you have, from fleeting acquaintances to your most intimate relationships.

9.1 THE MOST IMPORTANT RELATIONSHIP: YOU WITH YOU

Imagine for a moment that you are two people: the You who navigates the world and the You who cheers on from the sidelines. How well do these two Yous get along? Are they supportive pals, or do they bicker like old rivals? The heart of all your relationships doesn't start with anyone else; it starts right here, between these two Yous. This foundational relationship with yourself is the bedrock on which all other relationships are built. If the rapport between these two Yous is strong, it's like having a built-in cheerleader for every other relationship you form. If it's fraught, every external relationship feels just a bit off-kilter, like a door that won't shut right no matter how hard you slam it.

This internal harmony or discord profoundly influences how you grow and connect with others. By cultivating a nurturing relationship with yourself, filled with acceptance and compassion, you pave the way for deep and expansive growth. As you tend to this garden of self-understanding, you start to appreciate your motives, fears and desires more deeply. This heightened awareness fosters more meaningful connections with others and ensures that these relationships are rooted in authenticity rather than necessity or convenience. Imagine navigating social interactions not as a chameleon, changing colors to suit the company, but as a well-rooted tree, steadfast in its identity yet flexible enough to sway with the wind. This is the power of self-love, empowering you to be your authentic self in every interaction.

Forgiving oneself is one of the most challenging rows to hoe in this garden of self-love. We've all got a closet full of skeletons that love to dance around at two a.m. when we're trying to sleep. Yet, embracing self-compassion allows you to look at these skeletons, acknowledge them, and then gently close the door. It's about recognizing that mistakes are not roadblocks but rather stepping stones on the path of growth. This gentle forgiveness liberates you from the chains of past regrets and empowers you to embrace future challenges with open arms, knowing that each experience, good or bad, contributes to the mosaic of who you are. It's a hopeful reminder that self-forgiveness is a key to personal growth and transformation.

Encouraging regular self-reflection and self-care isn't about indulging oneself; it's a critical practice of tuning in to your needs and desires. Think of it as regular check-ins at a favorite coffee shop with an old friend—yourself. This could be as simple as setting aside time each week to journal, meditate, or engage in an activity that rejuvenates your spirit. These moments of introspection and care reinforce the importance of your relationship with yourself, ensuring it remains vibrant and nourished.

Interactive Element: Your Self-Love Playlist

Create a playlist of songs that make you feel empowered, understood, or just plain happy. Music has a profound ability to affect our moods and outlook. Each track you choose should resonate with a facet of your personality or a milestone in your self-love journey. Play this setlist during your self-care rituals or when you need a reminder of how far you've come in your relationship with yourself. This personalized soundtrack can become a musical journal of your journey toward deeper self-love and understanding.

In weaving these practices of self-understanding, self-compassion, and regular self-care into the fabric of your daily life, you are enhancing your relationship with yourself and setting a pattern for healthier, more fulfilling interactions with others. Just like those carefree moments of singing into your shampoo bottle, embracing and nurturing the relationship with yourself should be liberating, joyful, and deeply affirming.

9.2 FROM SELF TO OTHERS: HOW SELF-LOVE IMPROVES RELATIONSHIPS

Have you ever noticed how the vibe you carry after a splendid self-care day—maybe after treating yourself to a cozy read by the fireplace or a peaceful walk in the park—changes your outlook and how you connect with others? It's like you're radiating a kind of sunny energy that makes conversations flow smoother and interactions feel lighter. This isn't just a feel-good theory; it's the ripple effect of self-love, profoundly impacting every relationship you have.

Let's unpack this. Think about how a strong sense of self-love influences your expectations in relationships. When you truly value yourself, you naturally expect others to treat you with respect and kindness. This isn't about demanding perfection from every interaction but about having a clear sense of what you deserve and what you don't. For example, if you've spent the morning affirming your worth, you're less likely to tolerate dismissive behavior later in the day because, well, you know you deserve better. It's like setting the price tag on your personal stock high because you recognize its value.

Now, consider how self-love shapes your boundaries. Knowing your worth helps you draw these lines more confidently. You understand where you end and where others begin, which means you can say no with less guilt. You realize that saying no to a late-night call from a friend who consistently drains your energy isn't selfish; it's necessary for your well-being. These boundaries aren't walls to keep people out; they're gates that allow you to control what influences you let into your life, ensuring that your emotional garden thrives.

Communication is another area where self-love leaves its mark. You communicate more openly and honestly when you're good with who you are. There's no need for pretenses or masks because you're not trying to make everyone like you. This authenticity also invites others to be real with you, paving the way for deeper, more meaningful connections. Imagine how liberating it feels when you can share your thoughts and feelings without fear of judgment because you've already accepted yourself. It encourages a similar openness in others, creating a rich, sincere dialogue.

Let's talk about the beautiful reciprocity between self-love and loving others. It might seem counterintuitive, but the more love you have for yourself, the more you have to offer others. It's not a finite vessel; it's an ever-expanding wellspring. This kind of love is healthy, not needy. It doesn't cling out of fear of loneliness; it embraces out of a desire for genuine connection. When you love yourself, you're more patient, understanding, and forgiving with others, recognizing that they, too, are on their own paths.

9.3 LOVE AND LET LOVE: ACCEPTING LOVE FROM OTHERS.

Have you ever found yourself cringing away from genuine compliments or feeling unworthy of someone's affection or kindness? It's like every time someone tries to hand you a bouquet of love or appreciation, you're convinced it's laced with hidden thorns. This struggle isn't just about modesty; it's often rooted in deeper issues of self-esteem or shadowed by past experiences where trust was as fragile as glass. Embracing love from others requires not just open arms but an open heart—one that believes in its own worthiness of love.

The path to accepting love is paved with vulnerability, a term that might make you wince a bit. Let's face it, being vulnerable feels like walking into a room full of strangers in your pajamas—not the most comfortable scenario. Yet, it's this emotional openness that acts as a bridge between hearts. Vulnerability isn't about weakness but courage—the bravery to let someone see you as you are, battle scars and all. When you shield yourself from vulnerability, you're also barricading your heart from the warmth of genuine connections. Think about the last time someone offered you a sincere compliment or a thoughtful gesture. Did you deflect it with a self-deprecating joke or a dismissive shrug? While it might seem like you're just being humble, deep down, it could be a sign of reluctance to acknowledge your own value.

Fostering this openness starts with dismantling the fortress you've built around your heart, brick by brick. Each brick likely represents a past hurt or a deep-seated negative belief about yourself. Begin by challenging these beliefs. If you think, "I'm not lovable," ask yourself, "Says who?" Look for evidence in your relationships that contradicts this notion. Maybe it's the friend who texts you every morning, the neighbor who trusts you with their spare key, or the colleague who always seeks your advice. These are not random acts of kindness; they are reflections of your worthiness of love.

Self-love is your ally in this transformative process. The inner voice cheers, "Yes, you deserve this!" every time someone extends a gesture of love. By nurturing self-love, you're healing old wounds and recalibrating your emotional compass to accept and enjoy the love that aligns with your true worth. This means recognizing that you are deserving of a love that respects and cherishes you, not one that undermines or devalues you. It's about setting a standard for the kind of love you accept based on the profound understanding that you are valuable just as you are.

Practically speaking, how do you start letting the good stuff in? Begin with gratitude. Instead of brushing aside compliments, try a simple "Thank you" and allow yourself a moment to bask in the warmth of appreciation. Keep a gratitude journal where you jot down acts of kindness and love you received. Over time, this journal can become a tangible reminder of your lovability and worth. It's a collection of evidence that argues against any self-doubt about whether you deserve love.

In embracing these practices, you're learning to accept love from others and to trust in the joy and peace that come with heartfelt connections. This trust enriches your life, coloring it with a spectrum of emotions and experiences that were perhaps previously muted by fear and self-doubt. As you continue to walk this path of vulnerability, gratitude, and self-love, you'll find that the world feels a little warmer, a little friendlier, and a lot more loving.

As we wrap up this exploration into the transformative power of accepting love, remember that each step toward vulnerability and gratitude is a step toward a fuller, more connected life. You are learning to not just give love but to receive it, to not just exist but to thrive in the rich, complex tapestry of human connection. This journey into love and acceptance prepares us for the next chapter, where we'll explore the joys and challenges of expressing love, turning our inward understanding into outward action, and continuing to weave love into the fabric of our lives.

Please refer to the "Journal Prompts" section at the end of the book and follow the prompts for Chapter 9.

CHAPTER TEN

CULTIVATING JOY AND GRATITUDE

E ver find yourself caught in a sudden downpour, and just as you're about to grumble, you see a child jumping gleefully in puddles? In that instant, your annoyance might transform into a smile. It's those tiny, often overlooked moments that can unexpectedly brighten our days. This chapter is your unofficial guide to becoming a joy collector in the vast museum of everyday life. Let's rediscover the art of noticing the little things that sparkle with joy, shall we?

10.1 DAILY JOYS: NOTICING THE LITTLE THINGS

Imagine starting your day not by groaning at the alarm clock's call but by celebrating the fact that you have a new day ahead. Sounds a bit like a cheesy motivational poster, right? But here's the thing: embracing this mindset can significantly shift your experience of the day. It's about tuning in to the small joys—the warmth of the morning coffee mug in your hands, the softness of your favorite sweater, or the cheerful chirp of birds outside your window. These moments exist; they just require your attention to be transformed into joy.

The practice of noticing and appreciating these snippets of happiness is like building a mosaic—one tiny piece at a time. Each piece might not seem like much on its own, but together, they create a stunning work of art. This is where mindfulness comes into play. It's not just a buzzword; it's a practical tool for tuning into the present moment. Think of it as a camera's lens, focusing on the details that make up your daily life. By cultivating mindfulness, you can start to notice joys that you previously walked past— perhaps too preoccupied with thoughts of the past or plans for the future.

Integrating Joy into Daily Routines

So, how do you make this practice a regular part of your life? Let's start simple. Each morning, as you brush your teeth or take your shower, challenge yourself to think of one thing you're looking forward to in the day. It could be as simple as a planned lunch with a friend or that new book waiting on your nightstand. This morning reflection sets a positive tone for the day, priming you to look out for moments of joy.

Another practical tip is to set little reminders on your phone or sticky notes around your workspace or home; they're like little nudges to pause and observe. For example, you could set a reminder to look out the window, take a deep breath, listen to the sounds around you, or watch how the light dances on the floor. It sounds whimsical, but these pauses can be incredibly refreshing for your mind.

Savoring these moments has profound psychological effects. Studies have shown that individuals who regularly take time to notice and savor the small joys in life tend to have higher levels of happiness and lower levels of depression and stress. It's like feeding your soul with little snacks of happiness throughout the day—each one nourishing and cumulative in its effect.

This practice also reinforces the connection between joy, gratitude, and self-love. Each joyful moment you notice and appreciate is like sending a thank-you note to the universe. It's acknowledging the abundance that exists in your life, shifting your focus from what's missing to what's present. And here's the beautiful part: the more you practice this, the more natural it becomes. Joy starts to color your everyday experiences, and gratitude becomes not just an occasional guest in your thoughts but a constant companion.

As you continue to explore these practices, remember the world is rich with simple pleasures waiting to be noticed. Whether it's the satisfying click of your keyboard, the laughter of someone you love, or the unexpected beauty of shadows on a sunny day, these are the threads of joy that, when woven together, form the vibrant tapestry of a joyful life. Let these practices be your guide, turning every day into a treasure hunt for moments of joy and gratitude.

10.2 THE GRATITUDE SHIFT: TRANSFORMING YOUR PERSPECTIVE

Have you ever had one of those days where everything seems to go wrong? Your alarm doesn't go off, you miss the bus, and then you spill coffee on your shirt. It's easy to spiral down into a mood where everything looks bleak. But what if, amidst this chaos, you could flip a switch in your mind that changes your focus from what went wrong to what's going right? That's the power of gratitude. It's not just about saying "thank you" when someone holds the door open for you; it's a transformative practice that shifts your perspective from scarcity to abundance, turning every day into a treasure trove of blessings.

Gratitude is like a muscle—the more you use it, the stronger it gets. But how do you start? One effective way is by keeping a gratitude journal. This isn't just any diary; it's a dedicated space where you record everything you're thankful for. Start with simple things:

- The warmth of the sun on a chilly day.
- A message from a friend.
- You had a delicious lunch.

The act of writing these down shifts your focus from what's missing in your life to the abundance that's already there. Over time, this practice can significantly enhance your sense of contentment and happiness.

But let's get real; feeling grateful is not always easy. On tough days, when everything seems to be falling apart, finding things to be thankful for can feel almost impossible. This is where the real work of gratitude lies. Try to step back and view your situation from a different angle in these moments. Ask yourself, "What can I learn from this?" or "Is there something I can be grateful for in this situation?" Sometimes, it's the hard lessons that bring the most significant growth. And remember, gratitude isn't about denying or glossing over the challenging parts of life; it's about finding a sliver of silver lining in the storm clouds, which can sometimes make all the difference.

Research backs up the benefits of this practice, showing that people who regularly express gratitude have better mental health, experience better sleep, and maintain stronger relationships. It's because gratitude helps rewire your brain to focus on positivity, which enhances your overall well-being. It acts as a buffer against stress and can deepen your connections. When you express gratitude toward someone, you're boosting your happiness and strengthening your bond with that person. It's a beautiful cycle: gratitude breeds happiness, which fosters more gratitude.

Of course, maintaining a consistent practice of gratitude isn't without its challenges, especially when life throws curveballs your way. In these moments, it's helpful to have a few strategies up your sleeve. For instance, integrating gratitude prompts into your day can serve as gentle reminders to shift your focus. These can be simple notifications on your phone or sticky notes placed around your home or workspace with questions like, "What made me smile today?" or "Who am I thankful for right now?" These prompts can help pull you back into a mindset of gratitude, especially when it's feeling like a tough climb.

Embracing gratitude transforms more than just your mood; it changes how you interact with the world. It's like putting on glasses that help you see the colors more vividly—the blues of the sky, the greens of the trees, the myriad hues of everyday experiences. Suddenly, what seemed mundane becomes miraculous. This shift doesn't happen overnight, but with consistent practice, you'll find that gratitude changes your perspective and enriches your entire life, infusing each day with a deeper, more profound sense of joy and fulfillment.

10.3 CREATING YOUR JOY JOURNAL

Imagine having a treasure chest where you could store all the glittering moments of your day—those quick smiles, bursts of laughter, and flashes of realization that life is pretty fantastic. A joy journal can be just that: a personal repository for all your daily delights, big and small. It's more than just a diary; it's a tool for capturing and reflecting on the moments that bring color to your life, and in the process, it becomes a powerful ally in your journey toward sustained self-love and happiness.

Setting up your joy journal is the first step on this path, and it's all about making it resonate with you personally. There's no one-size-fits-all here; some might prefer a sleek, minimalist notebook that feels smooth to the touch, while others might go for something rustic with a bit of character, maybe even a hint of old-book smell. Or perhaps you're tech-savvy, and a digital journal on your tablet feels more your speed, where you can type, tap, and swipe your joyful entries. The key is to choose a format that feels inviting and inspiring to you. It should beckon you to come and scribble down your joys, not feel like a chore or another to-do item on your list.

Now, what to fill it with? This is where the magic happens. Start by considering simple prompts that guide your attention to joy and gratitude. For instance, you might write, "One thing that made me laugh today," or "A person who helped me in a small but meaningful way." These prompts don't have to be complicated; they just need to nudge you to notice and appreciate the sweetness of everyday life. You could also dedicate pages to more significant events or happenings that filled you with happiness, describing them vividly. This serves as a beautiful way to relive those moments and reinforces the feelings of joy and gratitude associated with them.

Incorporating creative activities into your joy journal can further enrich this practice. Maybe one day, you sketch a scene that made you smile or paste a photo of a spontaneous adventure with friends. How about including a pocket in your journal where you can tuck away movie tickets, dried flowers, or other small mementos that bring back joyful memories? These additions make your joy journal a dynamic and interactive scrapbook of your life's happiest moments, turning it into a deeply personal and visually engaging reflection of your journey.

Regularly revisiting your joy journal plays a crucial role in this practice. It's not just about recording; it's about reflecting. On days when the clouds roll in and everything feels a bit gray, flipping through your joy journal can provide a powerful reminder of the light in your life. It shows you that happiness isn't just found in monumental achievements or milestones but also woven through the fabric of everyday living. This habit of reflection not only bolsters your mood in the moment but also gradually shifts your overall perspective, helping you cultivate a lasting appreciation for life's joys.

With its collection of happy snapshots and reflections, your joy journal becomes a cherished tool for nurturing a positive, joyful outlook. It encourages a habit of noticing the beauty in the mundane and finding reasons to smile, even on more challenging days. This practice doesn't just enhance your days; it transforms your relationship with life, teaching you to cherish and amplify the joy that surrounds you, often waiting just beneath the surface of ordinary moments.

Let this joy journal be your guide and companion as you continue to explore the landscapes of self-love and happiness. Each entry, each page turned, is a step forward in your path, a path that is uniquely yours but universally beautiful. As you close this chapter, remember that recognizing joy is a form of gratitude, a way of saying to the world, "Thank you for this moment." Carry this gratitude with you as you step into the next chapter, ready to explore new depths of self-discovery and happiness.

Please refer to the "Journal Prompts" section at the end of the book and follow the prompts for Chapter 10.

CHAPTER ELEVEN

FACING AND HEALING FROM TRAUMA

E ver found an old, forgotten letter tucked away in the back of a drawer and, upon reading it, experienced a flood of emotions you thought were long past? Trauma can be a lot like that —old wounds buried under layers of time, still potent enough to stir deep emotions when stumbled upon unexpectedly. Many of us walk through life carrying the weight of these hidden traumas, often without realizing it. They shape our reactions, our self-esteem, and how we interact with the world. Acknowledging and addressing these hidden traumas can be the key to unlocking a deeper understanding of ourselves and embarking on a transformative healing process.

11.1 RECOGNIZING HIDDEN TRAUMAS

How do you begin to recognize something buried deep within, perhaps for years? It starts with tuning in to the subtle signals your body and mind have been sending you. Maybe you've noticed that you're unusually irritable on Sundays, the anxiety bubbling up like a pot left too long on the stove. Or perhaps there's a heaviness in your chest when specific topics crop up in conversation, a weight you can't quite explain. These emotional and physical reactions can be indicators of unresolved trauma, whispers of past pains echoing in your present.

Emotionally, trauma can manifest in various ways—sudden mood swings, unexplained sadness, or overwhelming fear, for instance. Psychologically, it might show up as persistent negative thoughts, an ever-present sense of doom, or debilitating self-doubt. Physically, your body might express its distress through chronic pain, fatigue, or inexplicable aches. Recognizing these signs isn't about finding a reason to label yourself as "broken" but about understanding more deeply what your feelings and body might be trying to communicate.

The importance of acknowledging these whispers cannot be over-stated. It's like recognizing that the smoke you've been ignoring is actually a signal fire, alerting you to deal with the flames. Acknowledging trauma is the first brave step toward healing. Facing those hidden shadows is an act of courage and also a profound act of self-care. By doing so, you begin to take back control from experiences that may have shaped you but do not define you.

However, uncovering trauma is not something you have to—or should—navigate alone. Seeking professional support can be crucial. Therapists, particularly those trained in trauma-informed care, can provide a safe space and expert guidance to help you explore these painful parts of your past. They can help you under-stand the impact of your experiences and offer strategies to begin the healing process. Think of them as skilled guides in excavating your inner landscape, helping you carefully unearth and address buried hurts.

Interactive Element: Journaling Prompt

To start this process, consider keeping a trauma journal. This isn't just any journal; it's a specific place where you can begin to map out when you feel certain emotions and what might be triggering them. For example, write about times when you feel unexpectedly sad or anxious, and note what was happening around you or what thoughts preceded those feelings. This can help you start to connect the dots between your current emotional experiences and past traumas, providing valuable insights for your healing journey.

Addressing trauma can indeed be a daunting task, and it's natural for someone to feel overwhelmed or even consider giving up when faced with the challenging emotions that can arise. However, it's crucial to recognize that engaging with trauma, despite its difficulties, is a vital step toward profound personal growth and healing. Here are some strategies that can help individuals stay committed to their healing journey, even when the process feels particularly tough:

1. Set Manageable Goals

Breaking down the healing process into smaller, more manageable steps can make the journey feel less overwhelming. Instead of focusing on large, ambiguous goals, setting achievable, clear objectives can help maintain motivation and make progress more tangible.

2. Seek Professional Support

Working with a therapist or counselor who specializes in trauma can provide essential guidance and support. These professionals are trained to help navigate the complexities of trauma in a safe and structured environment, offering coping strategies and therapeutic interventions tailored to individual needs.

3. Establish a Support System

Surrounding oneself with understanding and supportive friends or family members can make a significant difference. Joining support groups where others share similar experiences can also provide a sense of community and lessen feelings of isolation.

4. Practice Self-Compassion

Healing from trauma is not a linear process and can involve setbacks. Practicing self-compassion means treating oneself with the same kindness and patience one would offer a good friend. Recognizing and accepting that setbacks are part of the healing journey can help maintain self-esteem and motivation.

5. Use Mindfulness and Grounding Techniques

Mindfulness and grounding techniques can help manage and mitigate overwhelming emotions during the healing process. Techniques such as focused breathing, meditation, or sensory exercises can help anchor the present moment and provide a temporary respite from distressing memories.

6. Celebrate Small Victories

Acknowledging and celebrating progress, no matter how small, can boost morale and encourage continued effort. Keeping a journal of accomplishments and reflecting on the growth that has occurred can reinforce the benefits of the healing process.

7. Maintain a Routine

Establishing a routine can provide structure and a sense of normalcy during times of emotional turmoil. Incorporating regular self-care activities, exercise, and hobbies can improve overall well-being and provide necessary breaks from the intensity of trauma work.

8. Educate Yourself

Understanding the impacts of trauma on the mind and body can empower individuals and demystify many of the emotions and reactions they experience. Education can also provide insight into effective coping strategies and what to expect on the road to recovery.

9. Adjust Expectations

Recognizing that healing from trauma is a gradual process helps in adjusting expectations about the speed and ease of recovery. It's important to acknowledge that while the journey may be challenging, each step forward is a move towards a more peaceful and fulfilling life.

By implementing these strategies, we can find the strength to continue our healing journey, even when faced with the inherent challenges of addressing trauma. Remembering that each step taken is part of a transformative process that leads to greater self-understanding and lasting change can provide the motivation to persevere through difficult moments. As you begin to recognize and engage with your hidden traumas, remember that this process is about moving toward a place of greater peace and self-compassion. Each step is toward healing and transforming your relationship with yourself and your past.

11.2 GENTLE STEPS TO HEALING

Embarking on the path to healing after recognizing your traumas can sometimes feel like trying to navigate a dense forest without a map. You know you need to move forward, but the direction isn't always clear, and the journey is anything but straight. Healing is deeply personal and unfolds at its own pace. It's a process that calls for heaps of patience, a dose of self-compassion, and a resilient spirit. But fear not; think of this as drafting your personal roadmap with tools and strategies that resonate with your unique experiences and current needs.

Let's discuss some gentle, accessible first steps to take on this healing adventure. Grounding techniques are your first allies here. These are simple practices that connect you with the present moment, particularly useful when past traumas attempt to hijack your emotions. One basic grounding technique is the 5-4-3-2-1 method, which involves identifying five things you can see, four you can touch, three you can hear, two you can smell, and one you can taste. It's a method that anchors your senses in the now, pulling your mind away from distressing memories or overwhelming emotions.

Self-soothing strategies come next. These are ways to calm and comfort yourself when you're feeling distressed, akin to wrapping a warm, soft blanket around yourself on a chilly evening. This could be as simple as brewing a cup of your favorite herbal tea, listening to a playlist of soothing tunes, or practicing deep breathing exercises. The key is to have a toolkit of comforting activities that you can turn to, helping to stabilize your emotions and offer a gentle reprieve from distress.

As you integrate these techniques, building a solid support system is invaluable. This doesn't necessarily mean a vast network of people but a few trusted individuals who understand and support your healing process. This could be close friends, family members, or a support group where stories and experiences similar to yours are shared. Sometimes, just knowing there's someone you can call when the shadows of your past grow too daunting can make all the difference. They don't need to have all the answers; their presence and willingness to listen are often enough.

Professional therapy plays a crucial role in this process as well. Engaging with a therapist who specializes in trauma can provide you with tailored strategies and support. Trauma-informed care understands the widespread impact of trauma and the complex paths to healing. Therapists and coaches trained in this approach can help you navigate your feelings safely and constructively. They employ various therapeutic modalities, such as Cognitive Behavioral Therapy (CBT) or Eye Movement Desensitization and Reprocessing (EMDR), which have been shown to be effective in treating trauma. Think of your therapist as a guide in this healing forest, helping you to steer through the thickets and underbrush to clearer paths.

Throughout all this, it's crucial to set your own pace and honor your feelings and boundaries. Healing doesn't adhere to a timetable, and there will be days when progress feels slow or nonexistent. It's okay. Healing is not linear, nor is it always smooth. There may be setbacks, and that's part of the process. During such times, remind yourself of the ground you've covered rather than the distance you still need to go. Celebrate the small victories—a moment of peace, a day without distress, an hour where you felt genuinely present. These are the markers of your progress, the sign-posts that show you're moving forward, even if it doesn't always feel that way.

By taking these gentle steps—grounding yourself in the present, comforting yourself when needed, leaning on others for support, and seeking professional guidance—you're not just navigating through your healing; you're actively shaping it. Each step is a puzzle piece, and while the picture may take time to come together, each piece is crucial. So, keep placing them down, one at a time, with patience and faith. Your healing path is yours to walk, and each step, no matter how small, is a part of your journey toward a more peaceful and loving relationship with yourself.

11.3 SELF-LOVE IN RECOVERY: BUILDING BACK STRONGER

When piecing yourself back together after a trauma, self-love isn't just a nice-to-have; it's the glue that holds all the pieces in place. Imagine you're repairing a beautiful, cherished vase that's come apart. Each shard represents aspects of your being—your confidence, your trust, your joy—and self-love, which is what patiently and carefully puts these pieces back together. It's a process that not only restores the vase but can also enhance its strength, making it more resilient than it was before.

Cultivating self-love during recovery from trauma involves an array of strategies, each acting like a soothing balm on old wounds. Start with affirmations—they are powerful tools for changing the narrative in your head. It's easy to get trapped in a loop of self-criticism, especially after challenging experiences. Affirmations help shift this narrative by embedding positive, empowering beliefs into your subconscious. Try starting your day by standing in front of a mirror, looking into your own eyes, and saying something like, "I am worthy of healing," or "I am becoming stronger every day." It might feel awkward at first, like trying to pat your head and rub your stomach simultaneously, but over time, these words start to weave into the fabric of your self-perception.

Incorporating self-care routines is another cornerstone of rebuilding self-love. These aren't just pampering sessions; they are fundamental practices that signal to your mind and body that you are worth caring for. This could be anything from regular exercise, which helps release endorphins, to setting aside time for hobbies that light you up inside. You could rediscover your love for painting or start a small garden. These activities aren't just filling time; they're pathways that lead you back to yourself, allowing you to reconnect with your passions and joys and reminding you of who you are beyond your trauma.

Celebrating personal growth milestones plays a crucial role in strengthening self-love. Recovery can sometimes feel like a silent process, and it's essential to acknowledge every step forward. You may have reached a point where you can talk about your experience without feeling overwhelmed, or you've gone a week without a night terror. These milestones deserve recognition. Consider keeping a "victory log"—a special notebook where you record every success, big or small. Flipping through this log can be incredibly uplifting on days when progress feels invisible.

As we close this chapter on building stronger through self-love, remember that each act of kindness toward yourself is a step toward brighter days. These practices are not just about moving past trauma; they are about moving forward with a deeper, more compassionate understanding of yourself and your capacity to overcome challenges. This chapter sets the stage for the next, where we continue to explore the transformative power of resilience, guiding you to not only navigate but also grow from life's challenges, fortified by an unwavering foundation of self-love.

Please refer to the "Journal Prompts" section at the end of the book and follow the prompts for Chapter 11.

CHAPTER TWELVE
SELF-LOVE IN ACTION

Have you ever meticulously planned a vacation, down to the last detail of which café to hit for the best local espresso? Now, imagine if you put the same level of effort into planning your self-love practices. This isn't about scribbling vague affirmations on sticky notes (though those can be delightful!). It's about charting a course that integrates self-love into your daily life so seamlessly that it becomes as natural as breathing. Self-love is not a luxury, it's a necessity for your emotional well-being.

12.1 CRAFTING YOUR SELF-LOVE ACTION PLAN

Creating a self-love action plan is not just about setting intentions; it's about weaving those intentions into the fabric of your daily life. Think of it as setting up a series of small dominoes; each action you take knocks over the next, creating a cascade of self-love that flows through your day. The beauty of this plan is that it's not a one-size-fits-all approach. It's tailored just for you, fitting into your life's rhythm like that catchy tune you can't help but tap your foot to.

Let's dive deeper into what a self-love action plan involves and how you can create one that resonates with your needs and lifestyle.

A self-love action plan is essentially a personalized roadmap designed to help you integrate self-care and self-love into your everyday life. It's about identifying specific actions that nurture and support you and then systematically incorporating them into your daily routine.

Identifying Your Self-Love Goals: The What and The Why

Start by identifying what self-love looks like for you. This is your "what." Does it mean taking time to read, ensuring you get a full night's sleep, or perhaps learning something new? Once you've nailed down the what, delve into the "why." Understanding why these actions matter is crucial—it's the fuel that will keep you motivated. Maybe reading helps you unwind, or a good night's sleep leaves you energized and ready to tackle the day. Your reasons are your own, as unique as your fingerprint.

Next, let's get those dominoes lined up. Break down your goals into specific actions and routines. If reading is your chosen form of self-love, schedule it like a standing appointment. Perhaps every night at nine p.m., you curl up with a book instead of scrolling through your phone. Or, if learning is your goal, dedicate Sunday afternoons to exploring new skills or knowledge areas. The key here is consistency; these actions must be regular enough to become habitual, like brushing your teeth.

Flexibility: The Art of Pivoting

Now, while consistency is key, rigidity is its unwelcome cousin. Life is about as predictable as a cat on a caffeinated spree—sometimes, you need to pivot. That's why flexibility in your action plan is crucial. Suppose you've set aside Sunday afternoons for learning, but a friend drops by. Instead of viewing this as a derailment, see it as an opportunity to adapt. Perhaps spend half an hour learning something new together or shift your learning to another day that week. The goal is to maintain the flow of self-love actions, not to chain yourself to a rigid schedule that adds stress rather than subtracts it.

Simple Actions, Big Impact

Let's sprinkle some practical magic into your plan with examples of simple, effective self-love actions. These should be easy to integrate, no matter your schedule. How about starting your day with a positive affirmation? Right after you wake up, even before you reach for your phone, take a deep breath and say something empowering about the day ahead. Or, try the "one-minute rule"—if something takes less than a minute, do it immediately. This could be making your bed, washing your breakfast dish, or replying to a text. These tiny actions reduce physical and mental clutter and boost your sense of control and accomplishment. Remember, it's the small steps that lead to big changes, and each action you take is a victory in itself.

Interactive Element: The Self-Love Weekly Planner

To bring this all together, why not create a Self-Love Weekly Planner? This can be a simple chart where you jot down your self-love actions for each day, ticking them off as you go. It's both a plan and a tracker, helping you stay on course and visibly showing your progress. You can decorate it with stickers, inspirational quotes, or whatever makes you smile—make it a joy to look at and a symbol of your commitment to self-love.

Crafting your self-love action plan is like drawing your personal treasure map, where X marks the spot for contentment and well-being. Each step you plot is a step toward a more fulfilled, more joyful you. So grab your pen, chart your course, and let the adventure unfold, one loving action at a time. As you move forward, remember that this map is yours to redraw as needed, adapting and evolving as you do.

12.2 OVERCOMING OBSTACLES: WHEN SELF-LOVE FEELS HARD

Imagine you're on a hike through a beautiful forest. The path is smooth, the birds are singing, and the sun is shining. Suddenly, you hit a patch of overgrown brambles. You can't see the path; every step forward feels like a battle. Practicing self-love can sometimes feel just like this—mostly a beautiful journey. Still, occasionally, you hit some pretty thorny brambles. These brambles are obstacles like internalized negative beliefs, harsh criticism from others, or the everyday stressors that life throws at you. It's easy to feel like turning back, but just like with any challenging hike, the views at the end are totally worth it. Let's talk about how you can clear these brambles and keep moving forward on your path to self-love.

First up, those pesky internalized negative beliefs. You know the ones. They whisper you're not good enough or don't deserve happiness. They're like seeds planted in your mind, sometimes from childhood or toxic relationships. They grow into gnarly weeds that can choke out all your positive thoughts. Pulling these weeds out requires a tool called reframing. Here's how it works: every time a negative thought pops up, challenge it. If the thought says, "I'm not good enough to achieve my dreams," reframe it to, "I am capable and strong, and I learn and grow every day." It's like editing a document, swapping out the words that don't fit until it reads just right. This doesn't happen overnight. It's a process requiring consistent effort. But gradually, you'll notice those weeds aren't regrowing as fiercely.

Then there's the external criticism. Sometimes, it feels like everyone has an opinion on how you should live your life. Hearing negative opinions, especially from people you care about, can feel like someone's throwing rocks in your path. Setting boundaries is how you build a fence to keep those rocks at bay. When someone throws negativity your way, visualize this fence and remind yourself that their opinion does not define your worth. Politely but firmly, let them know you value their concern but are choosing to follow your own path. Remember, setting boundaries isn't about being defensive; it's about proactively deciding who and what you allow to influence your life.

Life's stressors are another type of bramble. Whether it's work pressure, financial worries, or just the chaos of daily life, stress can make it hard to prioritize self-love. Here, building a support network is like finding a hiking buddy. Having someone by your side is a huge relief when the trail gets challenging. This network could be friends, family, or even a community of like-minded individuals online. Don't be afraid to reach out when you're feeling overwhelmed. Share your struggles, listen to theirs, and support each other. Knowing you're not alone can lighten the load significantly.

Lastly, embracing the idea that challenges are opportunities for growth can transform the way you view obstacles on your self-love path. Every challenge is a chance to learn something new about yourself, to strengthen your resolve, or to practice kindness toward yourself. Every tough stretch of that hike is preparing you for an even steeper climb in the future. This perspective shift can turn a daunting obstacle into an exciting challenge.

Navigating through these brambles of self-love isn't always easy, but remember, you've got the tools to clear the path. With each step, you're not just moving forward but also nurturing a more loving, resilient version of yourself. So, keep going, keep growing, and know that every step, no matter how small, is a part of creating the beautiful landscape of your life.

12.3 CELEBRATING YOUR SELF-LOVE MILESTONES

Imagine you've just nailed a high score in your favorite video game or finally hit that tricky yoga pose you've been working on for weeks. The rush, the joy, and the urge to tell someone are the sparks of celebrating personal victories. In fostering self-love, marking milestones isn't just about giving yourself a pat on the back. It's about recognizing the significance of each step you've taken toward embracing who you are, reinforcing the positive changes you've made, and fueling your motivation to continue. These celebrations are essential checkpoints that remind you of your growth and the value of your efforts.

Think about the last time you achieved something in your self-love practice. Maybe you managed to say no to an unnecessary commitment, or perhaps you took an entire day for yourself without feeling guilty. These milestones deserve celebration. They are tangible proof of your commitment to your well-being. Creative and meaningful acknowledgment of these achievements can significantly enhance your motivation and dedication to your self-love practice. For instance, journaling about your achievements offers a reflective insight into what you've accomplished. It's like writing a letter to your future self, documenting the steps and hurdles you've overcome. This record becomes a motivational script you can revisit whenever you need a reminder of your capabilities.

Sharing your successes with loved ones can also multiply the joy of your milestones. It creates a shared moment of celebration that not only uplifts you but also inspires others. Whether it's a small gathering with close friends where you share what you've accomplished or a simple post on your social media sharing a moment of personal victory, each share is a ripple that extends the positive energy of your achievements. Moreover, treating yourself to a unique experience as a form of celebration can be incredibly fulfilling. Perhaps a concert of your favorite band, a weekend retreat, or a simple spa day. These acts of kindness toward yourself reinforce the importance of rewarding efforts, regardless of size.

Reflection plays a pivotal role in this celebratory process. It's not just about looking back at what you've done but understanding how each action has shaped you. Reflecting on your self-love milestones helps you to see the bigger picture—how far you've come from where you started and how each step has contributed to your greater sense of self-worth and fulfillment. This reflective practice deepens your appreciation for your efforts and sharpens your focus for future goals. It's like standing on a mountain you've climbed, looking back at your path, and recognizing the steep slopes you conquered and the obstacles you navigated.

Every step forward, no matter how small, is indeed a victory. In the grand tapestry of your life, these steps are the vibrant threads that add depth and beauty to your journey. They prove your resilience and commitment to living a life that fully embraces who you are. Celebrating these milestones is not just an act of joy but a reaffirmation of your worth and your journey toward a more loving relationship with yourself.

As this chapter wraps up, remember that each celebration is a cornerstone in the foundation of your self-love. These moments of joy and acknowledgment are vital in maintaining the momentum of your self-care practices, reminding you that every effort and every step forward is worthwhile. As you move forward, carry with you the joy of these celebrations and let them light up your path as you continue to explore, grow, and love yourself more deeply.

Please refer to the "Journal Prompts" section at the end of the book and follow the prompts for Chapter 12.

CHAPTER THIRTEEN

THE PATH FORWARD

E ver been to a concert, standing in the glow of the stage lights, feeling the music vibrate through your bones, and thought, "Wow, this is what joy feels like"? Now, imagine harnessing that electrifying energy every day. No, I'm not suggesting you haul a speaker around with you (though, if that's your jam, go for it!). I'm talking about channeling that vibe into envisioning a future where self-love isn't just on your daily to-do list—it's at the heart of everything you do. This chapter is about painting a picture of that future. In this masterpiece, the colors of self-love touch every part of your life, enhancing the hues of your daily experiences and interactions.

13.1 VISIONING YOUR SELF-LOVE FUTURE

Envisioning a Future Guided by Self-Love

Close your eyes for a moment—go on, really close them—and picture yourself a few years from now. In this future, self-love is not just a passenger in your life's plane; it's the pilot, guiding you through decisions, relationships, and personal growth. What does this look like? Maybe it's you turning down a job that doesn't align with your values despite the hefty paycheck. Or perhaps it's you choosing to spend the evening with a good book instead of that party you feel obligated to attend. Here, self-love isn't just an occasional visitor; it's the lens through which you view the world, helping you make choices that truly resonate with who you are and want to be.

Crafting a Vision Board or Journal

Let's get crafty with a vision board or journal to bring this vivid picture to life. This isn't just an arts and crafts project; it's a powerful tool to materialize your aspirations. Grab some magazines, scissors, and glue, and get clipping. Look for images that speak to your goals of self-love—pictures of serene landscapes for peace, vibrant gatherings for rich relationships, or serene spaces for personal growth. If cutting and pasting isn't your thing, sketch or jot down your visions in a journal. Draw your future self, map out your dreams, or script a day in your ideal life. This board or journal becomes a visual and tangible representation of where you're headed, a daily reminder of the life you're sculpting with self-love at its core.

The Role of Self-Love in Achieving Personal Dreams

With your vision board or journal at hand, consider how a solid foundation of self-love can empower you to chase and achieve those big, sparkling dreams. Self-love equips you with confidence —it's like having an inner cheerleader who's always rooting for you, shouting, "You can do it!" from the sidelines. This confidence fuels your drive to pursue goals that might seem daunting or out of reach. It's the difference between "I wish I could" and "I will." When self-love is your starting point, every step toward your dreams is taken with a spirit of worthiness and capability, inspiring you to reach new heights.

Setting Intentions for a Self-Loving Lifestyle

Now, let's set some intentions. Intentions are like setting your GPS before a road trip. They guide your actions and ensure you're headed where you want to go. But here's the kicker: these aren't just any intentions; they're soaked in self-love. That means each intention should support and reflect your commitment to treating yourself with kindness, respect, and understanding. Maybe one of your intentions is to speak kindly to yourself, especially in moments of mistake or failure. Or perhaps it's to carve out time each week to engage in activities that nourish your soul, like that yoga class you love or coffee dates with yourself at the local café. These intentions should encompass all aspects of your life, ensuring that self-love isn't segmented to one corner but is a theme that runs through everything you do, fostering a sense of self-compassion.

Interactive Element: Reflective Journaling Prompt

To deepen this visioning process, here's a prompt for your reflective journaling: "In a future guided by self-love, what are three decisions I see myself making, and how do these choices reflect my true self?" This exercise isn't just about dreaming; it's about connecting those dreams to actionable, realistic decisions you can start working toward now, even in small ways.

By setting these visions, crafting a tangible reminder with your vision board or journal, understanding the empowering role of self-love in achieving your dreams, and setting holistic intentions, you're not just daydreaming about a brighter future—you're laying down the blueprints to build it. And with each small action aligned with these visions and intentions, you're turning your daydreams into your everyday reality, creating a life that's as vibrant and fulfilling as you imagined.

13.2 SETTING GOALS WITH SELF-LOVE IN MIND

Have you ever set a goal that felt more like a towering, insurmountable mountain than a motivational milestone? Sometimes, in our zest to reach new heights, we sketch out goals that stretch too far above our current reach, neglecting the crucial element of self-love in the blueprint. Let's reshape that approach. Imagine setting goals that not only challenge you but also cherish you, reflecting your intrinsic worth and supporting your personal growth narrative. It's about crafting goals that honor who you are and who you aspire to be without putting your well-being on the back burner.

When you start to set goals with self-love in mind, it's like choosing to plant a garden you enjoy tending to rather than one that looks good to passersby. It begins with understanding that your goals should mirror your personal values and contribute to your growth, not just societal expectations or external validations. For instance, if creativity fuels your soul, setting a goal to complete a creative project each month can be incredibly fulfilling. It aligns with your personal values and feeds your spirit, making the goal meaningful and enjoyable rather than just another task on your to-do list.

Balancing ambition with self-compassion is crucial. It's easy to get caught up in the rush toward achieving our goals, pushing ourselves relentlessly. However, you must remember that you're a human, not a productivity machine. Self-compassion means giving yourself permission to rest, to make mistakes, and to go at a pace that feels right for you. It's acknowledging that setbacks are part of the process, not indicators of failure. For example, if you miss a deadline for one of your goals, instead of spiraling into self-criticism, offer yourself understanding and consider what adjustments might be needed to better align your goals with your current life circumstances.

Creating actionable steps for your self-love goals is about breaking them into bite-sized, manageable pieces. Suppose your goal is to improve your physical health. Rather than vaguely aiming to "get fit," specify actionable steps like, "I will attend three yoga classes per week," or "I will incorporate vegetables into at least two meals each day." These specific actions make your goal more tangible and achievable, reducing the overwhelm that can come with vague, lofty goals. It's about paving a clear, step-by-step path that gradually leads you to your more significant aspirations.

Regular reflection and adjustment of goals are essential as you evolve and your circumstances change. Just like a smartphone app needs updates to function optimally, your goals may need tweaking to stay aligned with your current reality and needs. Set a regular interval, once a month or once a quarter, to sit down with your goals and reflect on your progress. Ask yourself, "Are these goals still serving me? Do they reflect who I am and who I want to be?" If your circumstances have changed or you've gained new insights about yourself, adjust your goals accordingly. This isn't about backtracking; it's about fine-tuning your trajectory based on the latest maps of your life's journey.

By setting goals that honor your self-worth, balancing ambition with self-compassion, creating actionable steps, and regularly reflecting and adjusting your goals, you're not just chasing dreams —you're doing so in a way that deeply respects and nurtures your core self.

13.3 THE EVOLUTION OF YOUR SELF-LOVE JOURNEY

Have you ever looked back at old photos and thought, "Wow, I've really changed"? Whether it's style choices (admit it, we've all had questionable fashion phases) or personal growth, reflection reveals our evolution. Now, think about your self-love practices. Recognizing and celebrating this growth isn't just about giving yourself a metaphorical high-five. It's about seeing how far you've traveled on this path of self-appreciation and understanding the profound impact it has had on your life.

Reflecting on your growth in self-love is like flipping through a detailed scrapbook of your life. Each entry, each moment of self-kindness, is a snapshot of your journey. You may have started by setting small, almost timid boundaries, like turning off your phone an hour before bed. Now, perhaps you're confidently setting major boundaries, like saying no to extra commitments that drain your energy. These aren't just changes; they're transformations—a metamorphosis of your inner self. Celebrating these victories highlights the strength and resilience you've developed along the way. It's crucial to pause and really soak in these achievements. Throw a little party for one, complete with your favorite treat, or simply take a quiet moment to smile and soak in the realization of how much you've grown. These celebrations reinforce the value of your efforts and energize you to continue.

But as you know, life loves to throw curveballs. As you move forward, the landscape of your life will inevitably change, and new challenges will appear. Embracing these changes isn't just about adjusting; it's about thriving. This adaptability is where your foundational self-love becomes crucial. Think of it as your personal tool-equipped with all the self-care strategies, boundary-setting 'nces, and positive self-talk you've cultivated. This toolkit 'ou to meet future challenges not with fear but with confi-'stance, if a new job or relationship tests your limits, recall how you've navigated past challenges. Remind yourself that you have the tools and the strength to handle this, too.

Maintaining a commitment to self-love throughout your life is not about setting a course and sticking rigidly to it. It's about evolving with your changing needs, desires, and circumstances. It's recognizing that, some days, self-love means pushing yourself to go for a run and sweat out the stress. Other days, it's about curling up under a cozy blanket and reading a good book. This ongoing commitment means continually checking in with yourself, asking, "What do I need right now?" and then having the courage and love to provide it for yourself.

As you keep moving forward, consider this ongoing commitment to self-love not as a chore but as one of the most rewarding relationships you'll ever have—the one with yourself. It's a relationship that will challenge you, cheer you on, and cherish you in equal measure. It's a lifelong dialogue between your evolving self and the core of who you are, rooted in kindness, respect, and deep, unwavering affection. As you continue to grow and change, let this self-love be the gentle yet powerful force that guides you through each phase of your life, ensuring that no matter what comes your way, you have the love and respect for yourself that you so rightly deserve.

As we wrap up this exploration of your self-love evolution, remember that each phase of your life offers new arenas for growth, challenges to overcome, and fresh opportunities to deepen your commitment to loving and caring for yourself. In the next chapter, we'll explore how to maintain this commitment, keeping the flame of self-love alive and vibrant as you navigate life's continuing ups and downs.

Please refer to the "Journal Prompts" section at the end of the book and follow the prompts for Chapter 13.

CHAPTER FOURTEEN
BEYOND THE BOOK

E ver found yourself at a fantastic concert, completely losing track of time because you're so connected to the music and the crowd? Imagine channeling that vibe, that energy into every aspect of your life, especially your journey toward self-love. This chapter, my friend, is about amplifying that connection, not through speakers and stage lights but through the people around you and the community you build and engage with. It's about taking the solo act of self-love and turning it into a choir of supportive voices, each harmonizing to create a melody that uplifts and inspires.

14.1 STAYING CONNECTED: BUILDING A SUPPORTIVE COMMUNITY

Finding and fostering a supportive community might sound as daunting as planning a festival, but in reality, it's more like gathering a few friends for an impromptu jam session. These connections can happen anywhere and come in various forms in our physical spaces and the digital worlds we scroll through. Whether it's joining a local yoga class, finding a self-love workshop, or connecting through online forums, each space offers unique opportunities to engage with like-minded individuals who are also on their self-love journeys.

Imagine stepping into a room or an online chat where everyone is cheering for each other's growth and well-being. In these spaces, sharing personal stories and experiences isn't just encouraged; it's celebrated. It's like each person's story adds a new verse to a much larger song.

This act of sharing can be profoundly transformative. It's not just about unloading your struggles or victories; it's about resonance. When you share, you might find someone who echoes your experiences or offers a perspective you hadn't considered. This exchange can fortify your understanding of self-love and provide fresh, compassionate insights into handling the challenges that come with it.

Now, let's demystify the process of creating or joining self-love groups. If you're thinking, "Where do I even start?"—don't worry; it's less about creating a grand organization and more about gathering a few people who share a common interest in growing self-love. Start small. Reach out to a couple of acquaintances who have expressed interest in personal growth, or post an invitation in a local café or on social media to meet up and discuss self-love practices. You are also welcome to come join Willow.Cedar.Sage support group on Facebook or Instagram: @willow.cedar.sage. These groups can act as accountability buddies, where you motivate each other to stick to your self-love goals and share resources and techniques that have worked for each of you.

Speaking of social media, it's a tool that, when used wisely, can significantly enhance your self-love journey rather than detract from it. Think of your social media feed as your personal gallery, one where you curate content that uplifts and educates. Follow accounts that focus on mental health, personal growth, and positive affirmations. Engage in communities that discuss self-love and self-care openly and supportively. But remember, the key is engagement, not just passive scrolling. Comment on posts that resonate with you share your insights, and connect with others who are on similar paths. By actively participating, you transform your social media experience into a supportive tool, turning what could be a source of comparison and self-doubt into a platform for connection and inspiration.

In building these face-to-face or virtual communities, you do more than expand your social circle. You're creating a network of support that vibrates with the same frequency of growth and positivity. This network becomes a fundamental part of your self-love practice, a dynamic and interactive space that supports your journey and enhances it. As you engage with these communities, remember that every interaction is an opportunity to learn, grow, and deepen your practice of self-love. So tune your instruments, gather your band, and let the concert of communal self-love begin.

14.2 SELF-LOVE IN THE DIGITAL AGE: RESOURCES AND APPS

In this digital age, where our lives can often feel like they're under the magnifying glass of social media, finding sanctuaries online that promote self-love rather than drain it is like discovering an oasis in a desert. Let's talk about transforming your digital devices from sources of stress into tools of tranquility and empowerment. Imagine your smartphone, typically a hub of hectic notifications and endless scrolling, turning into a pocket-sized personal coach that cheers you on, reminds you to breathe, and provides you with pearls of wisdom exactly when you need them. That's the magic of self-love resources and apps—they're ready to serve you, not drain you.

Firstly, there's a treasure trove of apps designed specifically to foster self-love and mental well-being. Picture an app like "Calm." It's like having a serene sanctuary at your fingertips, offering guided meditations, soothing stories, and gentle reminders to check in with yourself throughout the day. Then there's "Headspace," which makes meditation as easy and accessible as grabbing a coffee. It guides you through the process with a friendly voice and clear, simple instructions—perfect for beginners and those more familiar with meditation. For those moments when you need a quick pep talk or a burst of motivation, "Shine" sends daily affirmations and articles that uplift and empower. Think of it as receiving a daily letter from a friend who always knows what to say to boost your spirits.

Online courses and workshops are fantastic ways to deepen your understanding of self-love. Platforms like Udemy or Coursera offer courses on everything from mindfulness to cognitive behavioral therapy techniques. These courses often come with community support, discussion groups, and even direct access to instructors through Q&A sessions. It's like enrolling in a university where all the courses are designed to help you become more loving and compassionate toward yourself. Plus, the flexibility to learn at your own pace means you can truly absorb and implement these practices in a natural and beneficial way.

Protecting your mental health online is as vital as safeguarding your physical health. The vast digital world can sometimes be a wild west of information and interaction. Creating robust boundaries around your digital consumption can help shield your mental peace. Use features like screen time reports to monitor and modify your usage. Be selective about notifications; only some apps deserve your immediate attention. Most importantly, remember that it's okay to step away. Just like you might close a book that doesn't resonate with you, feel free to close apps or even delete them if they no longer serve your path to self-love.

Integrating these digital tools and practices into your life transforms your devices from potential stressors to supporters of your self-love practice. Each app, each course, and each mindful interaction online becomes a step in your path toward a more loving relationship with yourself, facilitated by the very technology that, when used mindfully, has the power to support and transform.

14.3 LIFELONG SELF-LOVE: KEEPING THE FLAME ALIVE

Imagine self-love as a cozy, crackling campfire you've built and nurtured. It keeps you warm, lights up your nights, and everyone enjoys its glow. But as with any fire, you must keep feeding it; it requires attention and care to keep burning through all seasons of your life. This ongoing nurturing of your self-love isn't just about adding more wood to the fire—it's about adapting your methods to keep the flame alive, whether it's a breezy summer evening or a harsh winter night. As you grow and evolve, so do your needs and situations, and your self-love practices should flex to fit these changes, ensuring that the warmth of self-love never dims.

Let's discuss how you can sustain these self-love practices as you navigate different life stages and circumstances. It's like having a good playlist ready, whether cleaning your house, celebrating a win, or just needing a pick-me-up. In your twenties, you might find that vigorous workouts and social gatherings fuel your self-love. But as you move into your thirties or forties, quiet evenings with a good book or meditative walks might start to fill your self-love tank. Recognizing that these needs will change is crucial; give yourself permission to evolve and let go of practices that no longer serve you. It's not about being fickle; it's about being in tune with yourself.

Adapting your self-love practices as you grow involves a bit of creativity and lots of honesty. For instance, if you've always loved journaling but are no longer reaching for your notebook, explore new forms of self-expression. Maybe start a vlog or switch to digital journaling apps that might spark that joy again. Or perhaps you've always been a lone wolf in your self-care routines, but now you find that joining group activities brings you more happiness. The key is to stay open and curious about what makes you tick as you grow. It's like updating your wardrobe: what felt great in your twenties might not feel so great in your forties, and that's perfectly okay.

Reflecting on the role of self-love in lifelong fulfillment, think of self-love as the soil in which your garden of life grows. Just as nutrient-rich soil supports a garden's growth, a deep commitment to self-love nurtures a fulfilling life. It's about more than just feeling good in the moment; it's about building a life that profoundly satisfies and aligns with your true self. This might mean turning down opportunities that look great on paper but don't feel right in your gut, or it could mean prioritizing relationships and endeavors that feed your soul. Remember, a deeply fulfilling life isn't built in a day or a year but over a lifetime of choices that honor your self-worth and happiness.

Sometimes, though, life throws curveballs, making sticking to your self-love practices challenging. It could be a new job that consumes your free time or personal issues that leave you emotionally drained. During these times, recommitting to your self-love practices becomes more crucial than ever. Start small; maybe reintroduce one small self-care activity back into your day. It could be as simple as taking five minutes each morning to stretch or writing down three things you're grateful for every night. These small acts can reignite the flame of self-love during times when you feel it dimming. Think of them as gentle breaths of air that coax a faltering fire back to life.

In nurturing this lifelong commitment to self-love, remember that it's not about perfection. It's about presence. It's not about never faltering; it's about how often you choose to come back to practices that honor and nourish you. Like any good relationship, your relationship with yourself through self-love requires patience, understanding, and occasional adjustments. And as you continue to tend this relationship, you'll find that the warmth and light it adds to your life are well worth the effort. Keep feeding your fire, and watch as it illuminates your path, not just for a moment or a day, but for a lifetime.

14.4 WHEN YOU STUMBLE: RETURNING TO SELF-LOVE PRACTICES

Ah, the stumble—it's like tripping over that sneaky step on the porch that you swear wasn't there yesterday. In self-love, stumbles might look like skipping your planned meditation sessions, snapping at a friend when stressed, or falling out of sync with the practices that keep your mind and soul in harmony. It happens to the best of us. And while it's tempting to beat yourself up or wallow in a puddle of self-disappointment, let's try a softer approach. Think of it as tenderly picking yourself up, dusting off your knees, and finding your stride again with a renewed spirit and understanding.

Navigating setbacks with self-compassion is your first step. It's about treating yourself with the same kindness you'd offer a dear friend who's had a rough day. Imagine saying to a friend, "Hey, it's okay you messed up. You're human, and that's part of your charm." Now, try directing that gentle voice toward yourself. Self-compassion isn't about making excuses; it's about giving yourself permission to be imperfect and acknowledging that every hiccup is a part of your growth, not a detour from it. When you meet your setbacks with understanding rather than criticism, you turn a moment of self-doubt into a stepping stone for resilience.

Reintegrating your self-love practices might feel daunting, like restarting a workout routine after a holiday feast marathon, but it's all about taking that first small step. Start with something easy and soothing; perhaps it's as simple as taking five minutes each morning to stretch or jot down one thing you're grateful for each night. These small re-engagements serve as gentle bridges, leading you back to more intensive practices like journaling or meditation. It's not about overhauling your entire routine overnight but reintroducing elements gradually, allowing your self-love practice to weave back into the fabric of your daily life seamlessly.

Each lapse in your self-love practice, each stumble, holds valuable lessons. Like little puzzle pieces, they help complete the picture of who you are and how you grow. Maybe you skipped meditation because your schedule changed, teaching you the importance of flexibility in your self-care routine. Or perhaps a harsh self-judgment opened your eyes to areas where you need to cultivate more kindness. Instead of glossing over these lapses, lean into them. Analyze what led to them, what they felt like, and most importantly, how you can learn from them. This isn't about dwelling on the past but understanding your patterns and triggers so you're better equipped to move forward.

Forgiveness is your secret weapon here. It's the balm that heals wounds of self-reproach and allows you to move forward with a lighter heart. Forgiving yourself is an act of profound strength, not a surrender. It's recognizing that while you might have veered off the path, you can steer back and find new, perhaps better, roads to travel. Grant yourself the compassion and forgiveness you'd generously extend to others and watch as it transforms setbacks into springboards for growth.

As you navigate these stumbles, remember that each one is part of your evolving story, not a sentence of failure. They merely show that you're pushing, growing, and challenging yourself. They prove that you're trying, and in the beautiful mess of life, trying is a testament to your strength. So the next time you find yourself face-to-face with a stumble, smile at it, learn from it, and step forward with grace and grit, ready to embrace whatever comes next with an open heart and an empowered spirit.

14.5 THE ART OF SELF-LOVE MAINTENANCE: DAILY, WEEKLY, MONTHLY PRACTICES

Imagine your self-love practice as a garden that you visit every day, each week, and every month, nurturing it with the right amount of sunlight, water, and nutrients it needs to flourish. Establishing a self-love routine is like setting up a watering schedule for this garden. It doesn't have to be rigid; it just needs to consistently nurture the plants, or in this case, aspects of your well-being, so they grow strong and vibrant.

Let's start with your **daily** self-love practices. These are like watering your garden—essential and regular. It could be as simple as starting your day with a positive affirmation that sets a hopeful tone as you step into the day. Maybe it's looking in the mirror each morning and saying, "Today, I choose to find joy in small moments." Or perhaps it's spending a few minutes every evening practicing deep breathing to calm your mind before bed. These daily practices are small but mighty—they're the consistent drops of water that keep the soil of your well-being moist and receptive to growth.

Weekly self-love practices can be thought of as checking for weeds and pests, ensuring nothing hinders your garden's growth. This might involve a more extended session of self-reflection or journaling every Sunday, reviewing the past week's highs and lows, and preparing for the week ahead with a clear, centered mind. It could also mean setting aside an hour each week for a hobby you love, whether painting, hiking, or playing an instrument. This nurtures your spirit and strengthens your relationship with yourself as you dedicate time to activities that genuinely resonate with your soul.

When it comes to **monthly** self-love practices, think of them as adding fertilizer or new plants to your garden—something that enriches and diversifies your space. This could be a monthly "self-date" where you take yourself to a place you've wanted to visit, like a museum, a new restaurant, or a scenic hike. It could also be a monthly check-in with a therapist or life coach, which helps you reflect on your personal growth, address any emotional challenges, and set intentions for the coming month. These monthly practices are your chance to add something special to your routine that keeps the garden of your self-love vibrant and flourishing.

Now, personalizing these practices is critical. Your self-love routine should fit your unique preferences, needs, and schedule. It should feel like a custom-made glove—snug and comfortable, not one-size-fits-all. Start by identifying what truly replenishes and rejuvenates you. If you're a morning person, perhaps your significant self-love practices should take place at the start of the day. If you find nature therapeutic, incorporate outdoor activities into your routine. The idea is to tailor these practices to bring you the greatest joy and the deepest sense of fulfillment.

The importance of consistency in these practices cannot be overstated—it's the regular tending that keeps the garden thriving. However, life is unpredictable, and flexibility is just as crucial. There will be days when your schedule is overturned, or your energy simply isn't there. In these moments, it's okay to adjust your practices. Maybe your hour-long journaling session becomes a five-minute gratitude list, or your morning affirmation is a simple, heartfelt statement of intent as you brew your coffee. What matters is that you maintain the essence of your self-love practices, even in a reduced or adapted form.

Regular self-check-ins are your opportunity to assess the health of your garden. Set a reminder to check in with yourself regularly—how are you feeling? What do you need more or less of? Celebrate your progress, no matter how small, and adjust your practices as necessary. Maybe you've discovered a new interest that you want to incorporate into your routine, or perhaps you've realized you need more rest. These check-ins are crucial for aligning your self-love practices with your evolving needs and circumstances.

Establishing and maintaining a routine of self-love that includes daily, weekly, and monthly practices and ensuring these practices are personalized, consistent, yet flexible nurtures a rich, vibrant, and deeply nourishing relationship with yourself. Like a well-tended garden, your well-being will flourish, providing a steady source of strength, joy, and peace no matter what life brings.

14.6 EMBRACING CHANGE: WHEN LIFE SHIFTS

Imagine your life as a series of musical notes, each representing different phases, experiences, and emotions. Now, think about how a sudden key change can transform a simple melody, adding depth and a new perspective to the tune. Similarly, life throws us into new keys without warning—whether it's moving to a new city, changing careers, or entering or leaving a relationship. These changes, while often exciting, can also be disorienting, making it feel like you're learning to dance to an entirely new rhythm. Adapting your self-love practices during these times isn't just about keeping the rhythm; it's about moving gracefully into this new dance of life, ensuring that your self-love doesn't miss a beat.

When significant life changes occur, it's like someone's turned the lights off in a room you thought you knew well, and you need to navigate it anew. This is where tweaking your self-love practices comes into play, shining a flashlight that guides you through. Perhaps your morning meditation no longer fits into an earlier, more hectic schedule or busy commutes now replace your long reflective walks. It's okay to reshape these practices. Maybe your meditation becomes a brief mindfulness session during your commute, and your walks turn into weekend explorations of your new neighborhood. The key is to maintain the essence of your practice, even if the form changes. It's not about clinging rigidly to routines that no longer fit your life but about maintaining their core purpose—caring for and honoring yourself amidst the flux.

Seeing change as an opportunity for growth is like spotting a sunrise on the horizon—a promise of new beginnings and fresh possibilities. With every major shift in your life, you can rediscover yourself and explore facets you might not have known before. It's about asking, "What can this new chapter teach me?" rather than, "Why has this change disrupted my life?" For instance, if moving to a new city makes you feel unmoored, it might also be an opportunity to develop resilience and independence, discover new hobbies, or make new friendships that reflect your current passions and interests. Each change and shift is a stepping stone to adapt and thrive, using the foundation of self-love you've built to explore these uncharted waters.

Maintaining self-love amidst uncertainty is akin to keeping your balance in choppy waters. Here, your self-love practices become your anchor, preventing you from being swept away by the tides of change. Having non-negotiables in your self-care routine is crucial —practices you hold sacred, no matter how the seas churn. This might mean ensuring you always have a quiet morning coffee, regardless of your day, or unwinding with a book each night, no matter how late you get home. These anchors hold you steady, providing a sense of continuity and security even when everything else is in flux.

In a constantly changing world, your commitment to self-love is a constant—a lighthouse guiding you home, no matter how stormy it gets. Remember, as the scenery of your life changes, the path of self-love isn't a straight line but a series of ebbs and flows. Embrace each shift and turn with open arms and a trusting heart, knowing that with self-love as your compass, you can navigate through anything life plays your way. As you continue to dance to this ever-changing melody of life, let self-love choreograph your steps, turning each new rhythm into a chance to grow, shine, and embrace the ever-evolving dance that is life.

14.7 PAYING IT FORWARD: SHARING YOUR JOURNEY

Imagine your self-love journey as a series of lightbulb moments, each sparking insights and realizations illuminating your path. Now, think about the power of sharing those sparks with others. Each time you share your experiences, it's like lighting a candle for someone else, helping brighten their path with the wisdom and lessons you've gathered. This sharing does more than just spread light; it creates a warmth that fosters a richer, more inclusive culture of self-love and acceptance, making the world a little brighter for all of us.

When you open up about your own explorations and challenges in self-love, you do more than recount your experiences—you invite others into your world. This invitation can be profoundly impactful. It can turn the abstract concept of self-love into something tangible, relatable, and attainable. Think about how powerful it can be to hear someone say, "I've been there. I struggled, I stumbled, but here's how I found my way." It's comforting and incredibly motivating. Your story could be the nudge someone needs to start or persist on their own self-love path.

So, how do you go about sharing these personal tales? Well, the avenues are as diverse as the stories themselves. If you're the type who loves a heart-to-heart, personal conversations can be a wonderful way to connect. These can happen anywhere—at a coffee shop, during a walk in the park, or even curled up on your living room couch. For those who are a bit more tech-savvy or literary, blogging offers a platform to reach a broader audience. It allows you to weave your narrative into posts that share your journey and invite feedback and interaction. If standing in the spotlight is where you shine, consider speaking engagements at workshops or conferences focused on personal development and wellness. These forums can amplify your voice and story, reaching ears eager for guidance and inspiration.

Now, consider the ripple effect of sharing your journey. Each person touched by your story carries a spark from it, potentially passing it along to others in their circles. This ripple effect can foster a widespread culture of self-love, where more and more people feel empowered to embark on their own self-care adventures. It's like planting seeds of empowerment and watching as they grow into a lush forest of self-love advocates and practitioners. This growth enriches individual lives and cultivates a community where support and encouragement are abundant, and self-love is celebrated and uplifted.

Supporting others in their self-love adventures can be incredibly rewarding. It's one thing to navigate your own path, but guiding someone else on theirs adds an extra layer of fulfillment. Start by being a compassionate listener. Often, what someone needs most is just to be heard without judgment. Offer the insights you've gained from your experiences, but remember, it's not about prescribing a one-size-fits-all solution. Please encourage them to find practices that resonate with their unique selves. If you're part of a self-love group, invite them along. Knowing there's a community they can turn to can make all the difference.

In sharing your journey and supporting others in theirs, you do more than just contribute to individual growth—you help weave a tapestry of communal well-being that strengthens the fabric of society. Each story shared, each hand extended in support, adds a thread to this tapestry, enriching it with diversity, strength, and beauty. So keep sharing, supporting, and watching as the world around you transforms, one self-love story at a time.

14.8 THE NEXT CHAPTER: CONTINUING YOUR EDUCATION IN SELF-LOVE

If you've ever tried to bake a cake, you know the joy of watching simple ingredients transform into something delightful—it's a bit magical. Think of your self-love as that cake. You've already mixed in some essential ingredients like kindness, patience, and resilience. Now, it's about keeping that baker's spirit alive, continually learning new recipes and techniques to make your self-love even more delicious and fulfilling as time passes. Lifelong learning in self-love isn't just nice to have; it's the yeast that makes your personal growth rise, expanding your understanding and practices in ways that continually renew and enrich your life.

Let's start by curating a library of resources because who doesn't like a good shelf of life-enhancing books or a playlist of inspiring podcasts? Imagine a bookshelf in your room, each book offering a different perspective on self-love—from psychological insights to personal memoirs about growth and healing. Titles like *The Gifts of Imperfection* by Brené Brown, which dives into the power of embracing your true self, flaws and all, or *You Are a Badass* by Jen Sincero, a cheeky yet profound take on owning your awesomeness and creating a life you love. These books don't just occupy physical space; they expand your self-love practice's mental and emotional landscapes.

Switching gears to podcasts, consider them conversations with wise friends who bring you insights and stories through your headphones. *The Good Life Project* offers heartfelt discussions that encourage you to live more meaningfully, while *On Being* with Krista Tippett dives deep into the philosophical aspects of personal growth and resilience. These podcasts can accompany you on a lazy Sunday afternoon or during a morning jog, weaving ideas and inspirations into the fabric of your daily life.

Now, let's talk about stirring in some new flavors to keep your self-love fresh and exciting. Have you ever added a pinch of something unexpected to a recipe, maybe a dash of chili in chocolate? It's surprisingly delightful. In the same way, experimenting with new self-love practices can bring surprising depth and joy to your routine. It could be exploring art therapy, even if you think you can't draw, or meditative gardening, even if you've never potted a plant. Each new practice is an adventure, a way to discover hidden facets of yourself and new ways to show yourself love and compassion.

Remember, self-love isn't a static, one-time achievement. It's more like a river, constantly flowing and reshaping itself. As you grow and change, so will your needs and ways of practicing self-love. What worked for you last year might not fit anymore, and that's okay. It's a sign that you're evolving. Embrace this change. Let your self-love practices evolve with you, adapting to each new chapter of your life with curiosity and openness. This continuous adaptation is not just about maintaining balance; it's about thriving, exploring, and discovering—continuously finding new ways to nurture and celebrate yourself.

So, as you turn the page to this next chapter, carry with you the excitement of being a lifelong learner in the world of self-love. Each day is an opportunity to learn something new about yourself, embrace change, and deepen your commitment to living with authenticity and compassion. Keep your mind open, your heart ready, and your bookshelf stocked. Who knows what wonderful recipes for self-love you'll discover next?

14.9 CELEBRATING YOU: A RITUAL FOR ACKNOWLEDGING YOUR GROWTH

Have you ever caught yourself in the middle of a regular day, and suddenly, a small victory from weeks ago pops into your mind, bringing a smile to your face? It's like rediscovering a forgotten cookie in the cookie jar—sweet, surprising, and totally satisfying. Celebrating your growth in self-love is akin to keeping that cookie jar filled; it's essential for reminding yourself of your progress and keeping your spirits lifted. Let's whip up a personal celebration ritual that honors your achievements and reinforces your commitment to loving yourself more each day.

Creating a personal celebration ritual starts with identifying what makes you feel acknowledged and appreciated. Think of it as planning your ideal party. What elements would make it unique? Is it being surrounded by friends or a quiet evening with a book and a hot bath? Your ritual could involve gathering a few close friends for a casual dinner where you share what you've accomplished and learned about yourself. Or, it could be as simple as taking a long walk alone in nature, reflecting on your growth and the hurdles you've overcome. The key is choosing activities that resonate deeply with you, making the ritual a genuine reflection of your tastes and joys.

The importance of acknowledging growth cannot be overstressed. It's not just about patting yourself on the back; it's about recognizing the real, tangible progress you've made on your self-love path. This recognition reinforces your efforts and helps cement the belief that you are capable of growth and change. Just like a gardener takes a moment to admire the blooms after months of tending, taking time to celebrate your own blossoming is vital. It's an affirmation of your worth and efforts, a nod to the fact that the time and love you've invested in yourself have borne fruit.

So, how can you celebrate meaningfully? Here are a few suggestions: perhaps you could create a "Victory Log"—a journal where you note down all your achievements related to self-love. Every once in a while, flip through this log to remind yourself how far you've come. Or, treat yourself to something special that you usually wouldn't—a concert ticket, a new book, or a day off just for yourself. These acts of celebration don't have to be grand; their true value lies in their personal significance to you. They are a way of saying thank you to yourself and acknowledging your dedication to your growth.

Setting intentions for the future during these celebrations is like sketching a map for the next leg of your adventure. It's about looking forward while honoring where you currently stand. This blend of reflection and foresight is powerful; it roots you in the present while keeping your eyes on the horizon. As you celebrate, ask yourself what new aspects of self-love you wish to explore or deepen. You may want to cultivate more patience or learn to set boundaries more effectively. Whatever your focus, let these intentions guide you gently but firmly toward continued growth and self-discovery.

As you design these rituals and celebrate your growth, remember that each small act of recognition and each intention set is a step toward a more fulfilled and compassionate life. These moments of celebration are not just pauses in your routine; they are integral chapters of your story, rich with meaning and ripe with potential. So throw yourself that party, write in that Victory Log, and treat yourself to those concert tickets. You've earned every moment of celebration, and each one is a stepping stone to an even more loving relationship with yourself. As this chapter closes, carry forward the joy and pride of your achievements, and let them light the way as you continue to explore and deepen your practice of self-love.

Please refer to the "Journal Prompts" section at the end of the book and follow the prompts for Chapter 14.

CONCLUSION

In concluding this journey through *The Self-Love Guide*, we leave not just with strategies but with a transformative new understanding of what it means to truly love and care for ourselves. This guide has not merely been a collection of techniques; it has been a gentle hand on the back, urging us forward into the deepest chambers of our hearts, where all genuine change begins.

Embracing self-love is not an act of self-indulgence but an act of rebellion against the voices that tell us we are not enough. It's a declaration that we will no longer be passengers in our own lives, driven by old wounds or the expectations of others. Instead, we choose to be the architects of our joy and the curators of our peace.

As you step beyond the pages of this guide, remember that implementing self-love is less about adding something new to your life and more about peeling back the layers of doubt and self-critique that have kept you from seeing your intrinsic worth. With each practice and act of kindness toward yourself, you are not building a new you. You are revealing the richness that has always been there, obscured perhaps but never absent.

Let this guide be your compass, but let your heart be the map. There will be days when the compass seems broken, when self-doubt clouds your path, but the map—the deep, unerring knowledge of your own worth—will remain constant and faithful. It's a reminder that no matter the challenges you face, your worth is unwavering and always within you.

Walk forward with the understanding that self-love is not a destination but a manner of traveling. Each step taken in kindness, every boundary set with compassion, enriches your journey, making the road less daunting and the scenery more beautiful.

Carry forward this powerful understanding, and let it infuse your every day and every action. Self-love is the quiet revolution that begins within and quietly transforms you from the inside out. Embrace it, and watch as your life unfolds into the most extraordinary of adventures—an adventure where you are not just surviving but thriving, rooted in the unshakeable belief that you are worthy of your own love.

JOURNAL PROMPTS

CHAPTER 1.

1. Beyond the Mirror:

- What does self-love mean to you beyond just taking care of your physical appearance?

2. Self-Appreciation Without Conditions:

- Reflect on how you treat yourself on days when nothing seems to go right. How can you improve the way you speak to yourself during these times?

3. Setting Boundaries for Self-Love:

- What are some boundaries you need to set or strengthen to better protect your peace and self-love?

4. Transforming Self-Criticism:

- Think of a recent situation where you were hard on yourself. Rewrite that scenario with a compassionate perspective.

5. Your Self-Love Definition:

- In your own words, redefine what self-love means to you now after reflecting on its deeper significance.

CHAPTER 2.

1. Rewiring with Kindness:

- Think about a time when being kind to yourself helped you feel better. How did your thoughts or feelings change after that?

2. Needs and Self-Love:

- Reflect on how treating yourself with love and kindness helps you feel more secure and happy. Why do you think it's essential for feeling good about yourself?

3. Bouncing Back:

- Recall a challenging situation you faced recently. How did being gentle and supportive to yourself help you handle it? What did you learn from this experience?

CHAPTER 3.

1. Self-Assessment:

- How do you react when things don't go as planned? Are you hard on yourself, or do you treat yourself kindly?

2. Reflecting on Influences:

- Think about a past event that significantly affected how you see yourself today. How did this event shape your view of yourself?

3. Celebrating Strengths:

- What is one thing you did recently that you're proud of? How did this moment make you feel about yourself?

4. Mapping Your Self-Love Journey:

- Create a simple map of your life areas (friendships, school / work, hobbies). Write down how you feel about yourself in each area. What parts need more attention and care?

CHAPTER 4.

1. What Are Your Flaws?

- Write about a flaw or imperfection you often criticize yourself for. Why do you think you see this as a flaw?

2. Flaws as Strengths:

- Next to each flaw you've written, describe how this could be seen as a strength or has helped you in some way.

3. Self-Talk Check-In:

- Think about how you talk to yourself when you make a mistake. What do you typically say? How could you change this to be more supportive and kind?

4. Fear Behind Perfection:

- Reflect on why you might strive to be perfect. Is it fear of criticism, or maybe fear of not being accepted? Write about what drives your perfectionism.

5. Celebrating Mistakes:

- Recall a recent mistake and write about what you learned from it. How did this mistake help you grow or improve?

CHAPTER 5.

1. Reflect on Resilience:

- Think about a tough time you recently faced. Write about how you dealt with it and what you learned from the experience. How did it make you stronger?

2. Define Your Passion and Perseverance:

- What are you really passionate about? Write down a long-term goal related to this passion. What are the small steps you can take to reach this goal? Think about how sticking to these steps can make you tougher.

3. Practicing Forgiveness and Grace:

- Recall a recent mistake or a time you were hard on yourself. How can you forgive yourself for this as you would forgive a friend? Write down a few kind words that you would like to tell yourself about this situation.

4. Resilience Journaling:

- Start keeping a daily log for a week, noting a challenge each day and how you responded to it. Reflect on these responses and consider how you can improve them next time.

5. Gratitude Practice:

- Each day, write down three things you are grateful for. Try to focus on simple joys or things that went well each day. Notice how focusing on the positive aspects of your day affects your mood and outlook.

CHAPTER 6.

1. Recognizing and Validating Emotions:

- Write about a time recently when you felt a strong emotion, like sadness or anger. What do you think this emotion was trying to tell you about your needs or feelings?

2. Journaling for Emotional Expression:

- Start a journal entry with "Right now, I feel..." and let your thoughts flow freely. Try to describe your emotions without judging them as good or bad.

3. Reflective Time:

- Spend some time thinking about a recent situation that made you upset. What was the real reason behind your feelings? Write down what you discover about yourself.

4. Cultivating Positive Emotions:

- Make a list of activities that make you feel happy and peaceful. Plan how to do these activities more often to keep your emotional garden healthy.

5. Emotional Gardening Practice:

- At the end of each day, write down one thing that brought you joy and one thing that brought you discomfort. Think about how you can have more joyful moments and what you can learn from the uncomfortable ones.

CHAPTER 7.

1. Redefining Self-Care:

- Reflect on what self-care means to you. List activities that you consider self-care and how they help you recharge physically, mentally, and emotionally.

2. Daily Self-Care Integration:

- Identify small self-care actions you can incorporate daily. How can these activities fit into your routine without feeling like a burden?

3. Personal Self-Care Plan:

- Draft a personalized self-care plan. Consider different categories like physical, emotional, and spiritual. What specific activities under each category make you feel cared for and rejuvenated?

4. Experimenting with Self-Care:

- Try a new self-care activity this week and journal about how it made you feel. Was it effective? Would you incorporate it into your routine?

5. Adjusting Self-Care Practices:

- Reflect on your current self-care practices. Are any of them no longer serving you? How can you adjust or replace them to better meet your current needs?

CHAPTER 8.

1. Time Management on Social Media:

- Reflect on how much time you spend on social media daily. Is it more than you intended? Set a realistic goal for how much time you would like to spend and think about how you can implement this change.

2. Feed Curation:

- Evaluate your current social media feed. Do any accounts make you feel bad about yourself or waste your time? Make a plan to unfollow these and find three new accounts that inspire or uplift you.

3. Critical Consumption:

- When you next log into social media, actively consider the authenticity of the posts you see. Write down your feelings about how real life compares to these curated images. How does this perspective change how you feel about your own life?

4. Digital Detox Plan:

- Plan a digital detox for a day or even just a few hours. What activities could you do instead that you would normally not have time for? After the detox, note any differences in your mood or productivity.

5. Setting Personal Boundaries:

- Think about a recent situation where you felt your boundaries were pushed. What was the scenario? How did it make you feel? Define what boundaries would have helped and think about how to communicate these in the future.

6. Dealing with Toxic Relationships:

- Reflect on your relationships and identify if any might be toxic. What are the signs? Write about how these relationships make you feel and plan steps you could take to improve or distance yourself from these relationships for your well-being.

CHAPTER 9.

1. Self-Reflection on Personal Relationship:

- Reflect on how you interact with yourself. Are you more of a supportive friend or a harsh critic of yourself? Write about how this internal relationship might be affecting your external relationships.

2. Acts of Self-Kindness:

- List three acts of kindness you can perform for yourself this week. How do these actions make you feel about yourself? Notice if these acts of self-kindness influence how you interact with others.

3. Self-Forgiveness:

- Write about a past mistake and how you currently view this error. Practice self-forgiveness and note how releasing this guilt changes your feelings about yourself and improves your interactions with others.

4. Regular Self-Care Check-in:

- Plan a regular "check-in" with yourself, like a weekly meditation or journaling session. How does regularly paying attention to your needs affect your overall mood and the quality of your interactions with others?

5. Self-Love Playlist:

- Create a playlist of songs that make you feel empowered and loved. Describe how each song reflects a part of your self-love journey and how listening to this playlist affects your emotional state and interactions with others.

CHAPTER 10.

1. Morning Joy Anticipation:

- Jot down one small thing you look forward to each morning. It could be something as simple as your favorite coffee or a chat with a friend. Reflect on how anticipating these moments influences your mood throughout the day.

2. Daily Joy Spotting:

- Keep a record of small joys throughout your day. These could include a pleasant conversation, a tasty meal, or a moment of quiet. How do these moments impact your overall day?

3. Mindfulness Moments:

- Set aside a few minutes each day to practice mindfulness focused on finding joy in the mundane, like enjoying the warmth of the sun or the taste of your food. Note how this practice helps you appreciate the present.

4. Gratitude Reflection:

- Write down three things you are grateful for at the end of each day. Reflect on how this practice shifts your focus from what's lacking to what's abundant in your life.

5. Joy Journal Setup:

- Begin a joy journal where you capture and reflect on daily delights and significant happy events. Describe how maintaining this journal makes you feel over time.

CHAPTER 11.

1. Trauma Recognition:

- Reflect on any physical sensations, emotions, or memories that arise unexpectedly or intensely. When do these occur? What might be triggering them? This can help you begin to recognize hidden traumas that are influencing your feelings and behaviors.

2. Trauma Journaling:

- Start a specific journal (or the back of a current journal) to document instances when you feel significant emotional shifts or unexplained physical discomfort. Note the context, your thoughts, and how you coped. Over time, this can help you identify patterns and triggers related to past trauma.

3. Grounding Techniques Practice:

- Write about your experiences using grounding techniques like the 5-4-3-2-1 method during moments of distress. How do these practices affect your feelings of anxiety or being overwhelmed?

4. Self-Soothing Activities:

- Journal about different self-soothing activities you try, such as listening to calming music or deep breathing. Which methods are most effective for you? How do they change your emotional state?

5. Support System Reflection:

- Reflect on your interactions with your support system. How do conversations with supportive friends or family members affect your emotional state? What kind of support do you find most helpful?

CHAPTER 12.

1. Identifying Self-Love Goals:

- Reflect on what self-love means to you personally. What specific actions represent self-love for you? Write these down and explore why they are important to your emotional well-being.

2. Planning Consistent Actions:

- Create a plan to integrate these self-love actions into your daily routine. How can you make these actions habitual, like scheduling specific times for them each day or week?

3. Adapting to Changes:

- Journal about a time when you had to adapt your self-love practices due to unexpected changes. How did you maintain your commitment to self-love during this time?

4. Simple Actions, Big Impact:

- Note the small self-love actions you take each day and their effects on your mood and overall well-being. Which actions have the most significant positive impact?

5. Self-Love Weekly Planner:

- Design a weekly planner where you can schedule and track your self-love activities. At the end of the week, review what you accomplished and how it made you feel.

CHAPTER 13.

1. Visioning Your Self-Love Future:

- Close your eyes and envision a future where self-love guides your every decision. What does this future look like? Describe a scenario where you choose self-love over external pressures.

2. Crafting a Vision Board or Journal:

- Create a vision board or journal that represents your self-love goals. What images or words will you include to represent your commitment to self-love?

3. Role of Self-Love in Personal Dreams:

- How does a foundation of self-love empower you to pursue your dreams? Write about a dream you could achieve with self-love as your guiding force.

4. Setting Intentions for a Self-Loving Lifestyle:

- What are some specific intentions you can set that reflect a commitment to self-love? List these intentions and explore how they can transform your daily life.

5. Reflective Journaling Prompt:

- Reflect on three decisions you see yourself making in a future guided by self-love. How do these choices reflect your true self and contribute to your happiness?

CHAPTER 14.

1. Community Connection:

- Describe your ideal support community. What kinds of activities and discussions would take place there? How would joining or creating such a community enhance your self-love journey?

2. Digital Detox and Engagement:

- Reflect on your current social media use and its impact on your self-love. Are there changes you need to make? How can you use social media more positively to support your self-love goals?

3. Resource Evaluation:

- What are three digital resources (apps, websites, online courses) that could help enhance your practice of self-love? Consider how each resource could be integrated into your daily routine.

4. Sharing Your Journey:

- Think about a time you shared your self-love journey with others. What was the outcome? How did sharing your story help others and deepen your own practice?

5. Long-term Commitment to Self-Love:

- Envision your future self, continuing the practice of self-love. What ongoing practices or habits do you see as vital to maintaining your commitment to self-love?

Join our community at Willow.Cedar.Sage on Facebook or Instagram to connect with like-minded individuals dedicated to their self-love journeys. Let's support and inspire each other as we continue to grow and thrive. Follow us to stay updated and engaged!

REFERENCES

Self-Love: A Short History of Self-Care & Self-Love https://www.asthebirdfliesblog. com/posts/history-of-self-care-self-love

The Five Myths of Self-Compassion https://greatergood.berkeley.edu/article/item/ the_five_myths_of_self_compassion

The Benefits of Self-Compassion in Mental Health ... https://www.ncbi.nlm.nih.gov/ pmc/articles/PMC9482966/

Love Gone Wrong: Malignant Self Love And Narcissism https://www.betterhelp.com/ advice/love/love-gone-wrong-malignant-self-love-and-narcissism/

The Neuroscience of Empathy, Compassion, and Self-Compassion https://www.sciencedi rect.com/book/9780128098370/the-neuroscience-of-empathy-compassion-and-self-compassion

The Theory of Self-Actualization https://www.psychologytoday.com/us/blog/ theory-and-psychopathology/201308/the-theory-self-actualization

The role of emotional intelligence and self-care in the stress ... https://www.ncbi.nlm. nih.gov/pmc/articles/PMC9756564/#:

Loving Yourself and Others The Impact of Compassion on ... https://www.vcuhealth. org/news/loving-yourself-and-others-the-impact-of-compassion-on-mental-health-and-wellness#:

Increase Clients' Self-Love: 26 Exercises & Worksheets https://positivepsychology. com/self-love-exercises-worksheets/

These 10 mental health goals will help you improve your ... https://www.calm.com/ blog/mental-health-goals

25 Self-Love Affirmations to Remind You of Your Worth https://www.verywellmind. com/25-self-love-affirmations-8553223

How To Start a Self-Care Routine (and Stick To It) https://health.clevelandclinic.org/ how-to-start-a-self-care-routine

Embrace imperfection: six ways to celebrate your flaws https://www.happiness.com/ magazine/personal-growth/embrace-your-imperfections/

48 Famous Failures Who Will Inspire You To Achieve https://www.wanderlustworker. com/48-famous-failures-who-will-inspire-you-to-achieve/

How to Practice Self-Compassion: 8 Techniques and Tips https://positivepsychology. com/how-to-practice-self-compassion/

Mindfulness-Based Cognitive Therapy: Benefits & Techniques https://www.verywell mind.com/mindfulness-based-cognitive-therapy-1067396

5+ Ways to Develop a Growth Mindset Using Grit & Resilience https://positivepsychol ogy.com/5-ways-develop-grit-resilience/

How to overcome self-doubt https://www.tonyrobbins.com/mental-health/how-to-overcome-self-doubt/

Evidence Mounts That Mindfulness Breeds Resilience https://greatergood.berkeley.edu/article/item/evidence_mounts_that_mindfulness_breeds_resilience

Gratitude: The Benefits and How to Practice It https://www.helpguide.org/articles/mental-health/gratitude.htm

Mental Health Benefits of Journaling https://www.webmd.com/mental-health/mental-health-benefits-of-journaling

21 Mindfulness Exercises & Activities For Adults (+ PDF) https://positivepsychology.com/mindfulness-exercises-techniques-activities/

Stress Management: How to Reduce and Relieve Stress https://www.helpguide.org/articles/stress/stress-management.htm

Research on How Mindfulness Changes the Brain (and How It Doesn't) https://www.mindful.org/research-on-how-mindfulness-changes-the-brain-and-how-it-doesnt/

Caring for Your Mental Health https://www.nimh.nih.gov/health/topics/caring-for-your-mental-health

The Difference Between Self-Care and Self-Indulgence https://mindoverlatte.com/difference-between-self-care-and-self-indulgence/

Self-Care For the Busy Person: How to Fill Your Own Cup https://www.metrofamilymagazine.com/self-care-for-the-busy-person/

The Radical History of Self-Care https://www.teenvogue.com/story/the-radical-history-of-self-care

Social Media and Youth Mental Health https://www.hhs.gov/sites/default/files/sg-youth-mental-health-social-media-advisory.pdf

How to Set Healthy Boundaries in Relationships https://health.clevelandclinic.org/how-to-set-boundaries

Toxic Relationships: Signs, Types, and How to Cope https://www.verywellmind.com/toxic-relationships-4174665

What is a Digital Detox? - WebMD https://www.webmd.com/balance/what-is-digital-detox#:

How Self-Love Can Improve Your Relationships https://myselflovesupply.com/blogs/blog/how-self-love-can-improve-your-relationships

The Benefits of Self-Compassion in Mental Health ... https://www.ncbi.nlm.nih.gov/pmc/articles/PMC9482966/

Setting Healthy Boundaries in Relationships https://www.helpguide.org/articles/relationships-communication/setting-healthy-boundaries-in-relationships.htm

How to Overcome Low Self Esteem in Relationships https://www.head-agenda.com/how-to-overcome-low-self-esteem-in-relationships/#:

Gratitude: The Benefits and How to Practice It https://www.helpguide.org/articles/mental-health/gratitude.htm

3 Simple Ways to Cultivate Joy Every Day https://www.mindful.org/3-simple-ways-to-cultivate-joy-every-day/

Why Keep a Joy Journal - Nexus Family Healing https://www.nexusfamilyhealing.org/blog/why-keep-joy-journal#:

How Gratitude Changes You and Your Brain https://greatergood.berkeley.edu/article/item/how_gratitude_changes_you_and_your_brain

Unresolved Trauma: Symptoms, Causes, Diagnosis, and ... https://www.verywellmind.com/unresolved-trauma-symptoms-causes-diagnosis-and-treatment-6753365

30 Grounding Techniques to Quiet Distressing Thoughts https://www.healthline.com/health/grounding-techniques

What Is Trauma-Focused Therapy? https://cctasi.northwestern.edu/trauma-focused-therapy/

My Story of Survival: Battling PTSD https://adaa.org/living-with-anxiety/personal-stories/my-story-survival-battling-ptsd

How To Create a Self Care Action Plan https://www.herbagswerepacked.com/blog/what-is-self-care

How to overcome self-doubt https://www.tonyrobbins.com/mental-health/how-to-overcome-self-doubt/

Celebrating Achievement - Recognize Success to Increase ... https://www.mindtools.com/ax3c2aw/celebrating-achievement

Personal Growth Through Self-Reflection https://bestdaypsych.com/personal-growth-through-self-reflection/

Self Love Vision Board: How to Create One In 4 Simple Steps https://occolondon.com/blogs/learn/self-love-vision-board

What is Goal Setting and How to Do it Well https://positivepsychology.com/goal-setting/

Give Yourself a Break: The Power of Self-Compassion https://hbr.org/2018/09/give-yourself-a-break-the-power-of-self-compassion

Self-Love: A Short History of Self-Care & Self-Love https://www.asthebirdfliesblog.com/posts/history-of-self-care-self-love

5 Effective Ways Community Spirit Can Boost Your Self Esteem https://friarymeadow.co.uk/community-spirit-self-esteem/

Digital Mental health tools: useful online resources https://www.cignaglobal.com/the5percentpledge/digital-mental-health-tools-useful-online-resources

When a Major Life Change Upends Your Sense of Self https://hbr.org/2022/01/when-a-major-life-change-upends-your-sense-of-self

The Power of Sharing a Personal Story https://www.thestorytellingnonprofit.com/blog/the-power-of-sharing-a-personal-story/

Made in the USA
Monee, IL
28 November 2024

71500772R00095